HISTORIC HAUNTS of the NORTH II

DR. JAMIE PEARCE

THE SEVENTH BOOK IN THE
HISTORIC HAUNTS SERIES

Inquiries should be addressed to:
Jamie Pearce
historichaunts@yahoo.com

BOOKS IN HISTORIC HAUNTS SERIES:

Historic Haunts Florida
Historic Haunts Florida II
Historic Haunts *of the* South
Historic Haunts *of the* South II
Historic Haunts *of the* South III
Historic Haunts *of the* North
Historic Haunts *of the* North II

Foreward:

  In this book I tried to include any and all personal experiences I had at each of the locations I've written about. Unfortunately, ghosts, as I like to say, do not perform on cue. In situations where my personal experiences were limited, I tried to interview people who lived or worked at the locations, past or present. Hours of research, traveling to the different locations, visiting, investigating, touring, and interviewing, all went into writing this book and I loved every moment of it!

Dedication:

I want to give a very special thank you to **Second Read Books** in St. Augustine Florida. They were the very first bookstore to carry my books. Since my first release in 2011, the owners have become like family to me. Much love Sue and Evelyn.
—Jamie

Another special thank you is to two amazing author friends of mine, David Sloan in Key West Florida and David Dominé in Louisville Kentucky. You two gave me so much advice entering the author life and you both have given so much support since the beginning. Big hugs to both of you guys!
—Jamie

My Historic Haunts series would not be possible without the support from the locations, past and present, and all the readers out there. Thank you so much for helping make my dream possible.
Hauntingly Yours,
—Jamie

Special Thanks:

Editing: Deric Pearce & Paula Dillon
Design and Layout: Deric Pearce
All images unless otherwise credited are provided courtesy of the author
Additional photography provided by and credited to original sources or Creative Commons.
First Printing October 2024/Copyright applied for

HISTORIC HAUNTS OF THE NORTH II

Table of Contents

CONNECTICUT
Humor & Haunts at The Mark Twain House & Museum...5
The Legend of Sleeping Giant............15

DELAWARE
The Battle of Cooch's Bridge,
and the Other Headless Horseman............20
The Paranormal Pea Patch............23

MAINE
Hitchhikers, Healing Waters, and Haunted Activity
at the Poland Springs Inn............26

MARYLAND
John Wilkes Booth and the Ghost
Whose Name is Mudd............31
The Mysterious Middleton Tavern............35

MASSACHUSETTS
The Spirits of the Joshua Ward House............38
Sea Food and See Ghosts at Old Yarmouth Inn............41
Spirits of the Spooner House............43
Spirits of Stone's Public House............47

NEW HAMPSHIRE
The Phantom Princess of Mount Washington............50

NEW JERSEY
The Haunting Tale and
Tragic Losses of the Hindenburg............54

NEW YORK
The Amityville Horror House..62
Apparitions and Paranormal Activity at the Ansonia....85
The Goblins, Ghosts, and History of Bannerman Castle...88
The Ghosts of Baseball's Past and Present.....................96
Legend of the Lincoln Ghost Train 103
Spies and Sad Spirits at Raynham Hall........................110
The Bronze Lady, Washington Irving, and
the Headless Horseman at Sleepy Hollow Cemetery........114

PENNSYLVANIA
The Ghosts of Farnsworth 117
We're Here! The Playful Haunts of the Inn at Herr Ridge..120
The Ticking Tomb..125

RHODE ISLAND
The Ghost of the Swamp Bride......................................127
Spirits, and a Master of Horror or Two,
at Swan Point Cemetery..129

VERMONT
The Haunting Story of the Hartford Bridge Disaster..138

WASHINGTON
The Exorcist Steps 141
The Haunts of the Unusual Octagon House................144
Ghosts in the White House..149

WEST VIRGINIA
A Paranormal Witness for the Prosecution,
The Greenbrier Ghost...154
Frightening Encounters at
the Abandoned Amusement Park....................................157
The Eerie Inmates of West Virginia Penitentiary.........163
About the Author 166

CONNECTICUT

HUMOR AND HAUNTS AT THE MARK TWAIN HOUSE & MUSEUM

The Mark Twain House and Museum,
Hartford, Connecticut

"Are we to be scared to death every time we venture into the street? May we be allowed to go quietly about our business, or are we to be assailed at every corner by fearful apparitions?...you are apt to think of spectres starting up from behind tomb-stones, and you weaken accordingly - the cold chills creep over you - your hair stands on end - you reverse your front, and with all possible alacrity, you change your base."
—Twain's "A Ghost Story"

Most of us are familiar with Mark Twain. We've probably all had to read one or more of his works in school, and enjoyed his signature humor. William Faulkner called him "the father of American literature". Even after his death he remains a fascinating man. One of my favorite actors, Hal Holbrook, performed for years on stage as Twain. His performances connecting many Americans to this great writer's story and history. Personally, I've always found not just his written works interesting, but his connection to unusual phenomenon and the paranormal. Many think Twain still haunts his old home in Hartford, Connecticut. If he is spiritually active, then it might have something to do with some of the unusual events he experienced growing up.

The Mark Twain House & Museum photographer Kenneth C. Zirkel courtesy Wikipedia Creative Commons

Riding a Comet's Coattails

Samuel Longhorn Clemens was born on November 30, 1835 in Florida, Mississippi. He was the sixth of seven children born to John Marshall Clemens and his wife Jane. He was the only one of the children born while the unusual astronomical phenomenon of Haley's Comet was high in the sky. The comet was thought by many to mark important moments in history (like the invasion of England by

Haley's Comet circa 1910 Public Domain Image

5

CONNECTICUT
Historic Haunts of the North II

William the Conqueror), or herald great things. Clement's mother claimed later that despite the fact that he was born sickly, the comet was an omen that he would go on to do great things.

Clemens Grows Up, Educating Himself, and Learning Trades

Clemens was raised in Hannibal, Missouri (the setting for **The Adventures of Tom Sawyer**, and **The Adventures of Huckleberry Finn**). Clemens would leave school after his father's death and after fifth grade to become a printer's apprentice. He would work as a typesetter, but also contributed articles and other works to the Hannibal Journal, a newspaper his brother Orion owned. At 18 he left Hannibal to work as a printer in several different cities, at night he would educate himself in the public libraries of the large cities he worked in.

Like many who grew up in Hannibal, Clemens harbored an ambition to be a River Boat Pilot. Steamboat pilot Horace E. Bixby took Clemens on to be a cub pilot, and teach him how to navigate the Mississippi. During his time on the river he became familiar with the cry of "Mark Twain", which was a term for a measured depth of two fathoms (12 feet). This was the safe minimum depth for a steamboat on the river. It took Clemens two years to earn his pilot's license.

While working to earn his license, Clemens convinced his younger brother Henry to work with him. He also got him a job on the steamboat **Pennsylvania**. On June 13, 1858 the boiler of the steamboat exploded. Henry was severely injured and died eight days later. Clemens never forgave himself for his brother's death. Regardless, he continued to work on the river until the Civil War broke out in 1861, effectively ending river traffic on the Mississippi.

Odd Jobs, Journalism, and Success as the Writer Mark Twain

Clemens followed his brother Orion to the Nevada Territory in 1861. After a failed turn as miner, he went to work for a Virginia City Newspaper. Here he wrote the first humorous account to which he signed his name as "Mark Twain". He moved to San Francisco in 1864 to work for a larger newspaper, growing more successful as a journalist and writer. The very next year he scored his first big success with the humorous tall tale "The Celebrated Jumping Frog of Calaverous County". Several newspapers funded him on trip in 1867 to Europe and the Middle East to write humorous travel accounts. While on that trip he met and befriended fellow passenger Charles Langdon. Langdon would share with Clemens a picture of his sister Olivia. Clemens would later claim that he fell in love at first sight with her after seeing her picture.

Mark Twain Finds Success and a Wife

Now writing as Mark Twain, he was first introduced to Olivia Langdon by her brother, Twain's traveling companion Charles. She was the daughter of Olivia

CONNECTICUT
The Mark Twain House & Museum

Lewis Langdon and Jervis Langdon, a wealthy coal businessman. She was well-educated and attended Elmira Female College in their hometown of Elmira, New York. Olivia Langdon (who preferred to be called Liv) went on a first date with Twain, attending a reading by Charles Dickens in New York. The two never met the famous author at the event (years later they would host his son at their home in Hartford). Twain and Langdon were engaged in 1869, and married in February of 1870 in Elmira, New York.

Twain Expands His Horizons, His Contacts, His Success, and His Family

Through his in-laws, Twain met and befriended Frederik Douglass, who the family had sheltered years before as a stop on the Underground Railroad during his escape. Twain's in-laws also introduced him to Harriet Beecher Stowe, famous author of **Uncle Tom's Cabin**. Douglass, Stowe, and others he met through his in-laws would challenge Twain's opinions on slavery, women's rights, and other issues. Concepts he blamed on a naive and isolated upbringing in Mississippi. Twain would become a strong advocate and abolitionist. Douglass and Stowe would remain dear family friends for years to come.

Mark Twain
Public Domain

Twain's writing, full of humor and wit, were bringing him increased attention and Twain and his new wife moved to Buffalo, New York to be closer to his publisher. The two were gifted a house there by Twain's Father-in-law. Unfortunately, Jervis Langdon would die 6 months later. Twain and his new bride welcomed their first child, a son, a short time after. Langdon Clemens, their son, was born sickly and premature on November 7, 1870. Sadly, like his grandfather, he died a short time later in June of 1872 from diphtheria.

Twain Moves to Hartford and Happy Productive Times

After a brief stint in Elmira necessitated by his father-in-law's death, and illness on his wife's part; Twain rented a house in Hartford, Connecticut. Twain was becoming quite successful and between that, and his wife's inheritance, they decided to build their dream house in Hartford. They selected a lot next to family friend Harriet Beecher Stowe. They also welcomed their first daughter, Olivia Susan (Susy) in 1872.

Twain's house was designed by architect Edward Tuckerman Potter in the American Gothic Style. Clemen's biographer, Justin Kaplan, called the house "part steamboat, part medieval fortress, and part cuckoo clock." The house was over 11,000 square feet, featured atmospheric interiors, and 25 rooms on three floors. It was equipped with the latest modern innovations of the time. In fact, it was among the first private residences to have a telephone. The family moved in to their dream home in 1874.

CONNECTICUT
Historic Haunts of the North II

Twain and his wife welcomed their second daughter Clara that same year (they would have one more daughter, Jean, in 1880). It was at their new dream home that Twain really got to work on his writing, especially in the Billiards Room. This room was off limits to all but the cleaning staff. It was here that Twain could be free to welcome male guests, swear, and to smoke his favorite cigars. In this room, his private study, he worked late at night. Twain wrote many of his best known stories here including: **The Adventures of Tom Sawyer, The Prince and the Pauper, The Adventures of Huckleberry Finn, A Connecticut Yankee in King Arthur's Court**, and many more. Twain and his family loved their time here.

Clara, Jean, Livy, and Susy
Public Domain

Twain and his family welcomed many of his friends here or corresponded with them from the house, friends like Ulysses S. Grant, P.T. Barnum, and others. Ever the fan of science and discovery (he held three patents), Twain became good friends with Nikola Tesla and Thomas Edison. Twain also met a young Winston Churchill, and encouraged a benefactor to aid Helen Keller (who also became a family friend). During the family's time in the house, their neighbor Harriet Beccher Stowe was like a fixture. She often let herself in to play their piano, pick flowers from their garden, and just enjoy the family's company. Through it all Twain wrote and smoked.

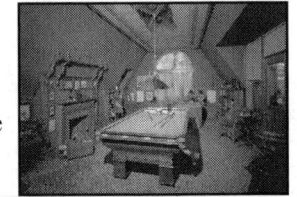

Mark Twain House
Billiards Room
Public Domain

Hal Holbrook
as Mark Twain
Author's Collection

Twain's Smoking

Twain had been smoking since before he reached adulthood. He preferred what he called only bad cigars, and smoked some 300 a month by his 30s. In his working heydays in Hartford, he smoked some 40 cigars a day! This was especially true when his creative energies were at their best. He became recognized for his signature cigars. He gave some of the his best quips and humorous comments when asked about his smoking habits by reporters and journalists…

"As an example to others, and not that I care for moderation myself, it has always been my rule never to smoke when asleep and never to refrain when awake."

"I never smoke to excess – that is, I smoke in moderation, only one cigar at a time;"

8

CONNECTICUT
The Mark Twain House & Museum

"Giving up smoking is easy – I've done it hundreds of times".
"If smoking is not allowed in heaven, I shall not go."
—Various quotes about smoking from Mark Twain

The Good Times Wouldn't Last

The family's time at their Hartford home was certainly their happiest, but the good times wouldn't last. Twain discovered he'd lost large sums of money to publishers in Canada and elsewhere that had printed and marketed his books without permission and profited greatly from it. He had to go to great lengths with frequent trips to Canada and other places to try to put a stop to this and secure his works. During this time, Twain also, unfortunately, made some bad investments. Chief among them a prototype typesetting machine that appealed to Twain and harkened him back to his early printing and typesetting days.

The obligations the family owed and the monies they lost forced Twain (now known worldwide), and his family to travel to Europe in 1891 to lecture, tour, and raise money towards their debts. They spent several years traveling through Europe. Fortunately for Twain, he was saved editing fees as his wife for some time had been editing his stories, articles, and lectures.

Sadly, still in debt, the family closed up the Hartford House in 1894. They declared bankruptcy in that same year and through some legal wrangling, aided by friends, Twain's copyrights were assigned to his wife (which saved the family's fortunes). Adding to their problems, Twain's wife Olivia and daughter Susy began to have medical issues.

In 1895, wanting to pay off his debtors and raise money for the family, he embarked on a world lecture tour with his wife and their daughter Clara. His daughters Jean and Susy decided to stay stateside. In 1896, while revisiting the Hartford House, and while her parents and sister were gone, Susy died in the house of Spinal Meningitis at age 24. The family was devastated!

Twain's wife could not bring herself to go back to the house where Susy had died. They remained in Europe for a time, before coming back to the United States (New York) in 1900.

Susy Clemens
Public Domain

By this time Twain had paid off all his debts. In 1903, they sold the Hartford home.

Unfortunately, Olivia's health began to decline and her doctors ordered her to move to Italy for her health. During this time she was to avoid anything that could upset or excite her. As a result she didn't see her husband for long periods of time on end and he was told by her doctors not to visit her and get her worked up. Still crazy about his wife, on numerous occasions he snuck in to share kisses and love notes. In June of 1904, Olivia died in Florence of heart failure. Again Twain was heartbroken.

CONNECTICUT
Historic Haunts of the North II

Jean Clemens
Public Domain

He moved back to the United States after his wife's passing to live with his daughters. In 1906 he founded the Fish and Aquarium Club for a group of girls he treated as surrogate granddaughters. In 1907, his daughter Jean passed from heart failure caused by an epileptic seizure.

Twain tried to take his mind off his misfortunes by once again lecturing and touring. By now he was a beloved icon all over the world and especially in the U.S. He was awarded Honorary Doctorates from **Yale**, the **University of Missouri**, and **Oxford**. By 1909 Twain seemed to sense he was not going to be on this earth much longer. He wrote the following,

'I came in with Halley's Comet in 1835. It is coming again next year, and I expect to go out with it. It will be the greatest disappointment of my life if I don't go out with Halley's Comet. The Almighty has said, no doubt: 'Now here are these two unaccountable freaks; they came in together, they must go out together."
– Mark Twain

Eerily accurate and prophetic as always, Twain died of a heart attack on April 21, 1910 with Haley's Comet in the sky, and still remembering his happy days in Hartford.

The Former Hartford Home

After the family sold their beloved home, it was repurposed many times. It served as a school, before it was later converted into an apartment building. The building had served for a time as a public library, something Twain would probably have approved of. Eventually, it fell into disrepair and was slated for demolition. In 1929, this historic home was saved from demolition by Katharine Seymour Day (the grand niece of Harriet Beecher Stowe). She recognized the significance of this building to the American Literary World. Monies were raised and the former residence began to undergo the restoration process in 1955.

In 1962, it was declared a National Historic Landmark. In 1974, it was opened as a museum—just in time for the 100th anniversary of the house—to help preserve the legacy one of America's most well known writers. Since then the building has seen another major renovation in 1999. A Visitor's Center has also been added to showcase Twain's life and works. The Museum has featured celebrated appearances by other iconic authors, many influenced by Twain, such as Stephen King, Judy Blume, John Grisham, and others.

In 2012, it was named one of the Ten Best Historic Homes in the World. Visitors today can enjoy workshops, lectures, and even guided tours and ghost tours. On some of these tours visitors have learned first-hand the possible connection between The Mark Twain House and Museum and the paranormal.

CONNECTICUT
The Mark Twain House & Museum

Twain and the Paranormal

It's no surprise that Mark Twain's former residence might be paranormally active. Restorations sometimes stir up this type of activity and the place has seen quite a bit. However, a better explanation for activity might be that of Twain himself. Throughout his life Twain repeatedly had run-ins with eerie and unexplained phenomenon. Because of this he developed a lifelong interest and fascination with the paranormal (my kind of guy). So much so that he joined the American Branch of the **Society for Psychical Research**, and the London Branch in 1885.

Still, Twain was a noted skeptic, and despite his family's beliefs in Spiritualism, persistently railed against the idea of ghosts. He went so far as to parody the idea of spirits in one of his own writings, "A Ghost Story". Still, he loved a good ghost story and loved to tell "The Golden Arm" repeatedly. This was a haunted folktale from his early childhood that spooked him.

Interestingly, several have suggested that based on his life and experiences, Twain may have been a "sensitive" himself. He maintained a strong interest in **Thought Transference**, what he termed "mental telegraphy". On numerous occasions he seemed to exhibit precognition. In other frequent instances, he exhibited a strange ability to "will" people to write, visit, or communicate with him more so than could be chalked up to coincidence. He could even eerily predict when they would write to him and what the contents of their letters would be before opening them, especially his close friends and family!

Touched by the Paranormal at an Early Age

While Twain was just a kid just outside of Hannibal, Missouri there was a strong belief among the locals of a sort of spiritual healer who lived just outside of town. She was a farmer's wife reported to have the power to cure maladies and illnesses, especially headaches and toothaches. The woman would place her hands on the victim's troubled areas and shout the word "believe" and the pain would go away. Twain's mother developed two bad toothaches during his childhood that left her with intense and overwhelming pain that she couldn't get relief from. In both instances, Twain was there when the woman placed her hands on his mother's jaw and shouted "believe". In both cases his mother was instantly cured of her discomfort.

Twain later encountered a fraudulent hypnotist working the crowd at a gathering at the age of 15. This left him with a strong desire to expose fakes and charlatans. It also convinced him that the mind may be capable of much more than most people realize.

The Prophetic Dream of His Brother

In 1858, while he was learning the Riverboat trade, Twain had a very vivid and prophetic dream about his brother Henry. In this dream he saw Henry as a corpse,

CONNECTICUT
Historic Haunts of the North II

lying in an open metal coffin, dressed in one of his own suits. On his chest was a bouquet of white flowers with a single red rose at the center. The coffin rested balanced on two wooden chairs.

Twain rushed to his brother in Memphis after the dream, and found him beside the rest of the wounded from the boiler accident on the steamship **Pennsylvania**. Unfortunately, nearly every detail of his prophetic dream came to pass in excruciating detail. All of the coffins for the dead victims of the accident were wood, except, strangely, Henry's, which was metal. Henry was wearing the same suit from the dream. Flowers were placed on Henry's chest and a strange old woman came in to place one red rose among them in the center. The only detail that changed was the placement of the coffin which would have been on two wooden chairs had Twain not intervened at the time and changed it.

Spiritual Connections Later in Twain's Life

Like his early childhood, Twain had another encounter with a spiritual healer years later. Olivia Langdon, Twain's soon to be betrothed, had become partially paralyzed after a fall on some ice. She had been unable to leave her bed for nearly two years. Any attempts on Olivia's part to raise herself up had brought her extreme nausea and fainting spells, and proved unsuccessful. Many reputable doctors had tried to cure her and failed.

The Langdon family contacted a faith healer known as Dr. Newton. Newton prayed over her and placed his hands behind her shoulders, raising her up. She rose, free from any nausea or urge to faint. After a few moments, she took several steps. Newton claimed she she'd never be fully cured, but would henceforth be much better. Twain was extremely grateful, because she could now walk down the aisle. She did so from that point forward and when they married in 1870.

Later Twain's daughter with Olivia, Susy, sadly passed. Afterword the family began to attend séances, and connected with mediums hoping to part the veil and contact her in the afterlife. Coincidentally, Twain's good friend, "the Wizard of Menlo Park", Thomas Edison, worked on his own "spirit phone" to contact the dearly departed. After Twain suffered the loss of his wife Olivia, he reportedly wrote several pieces on mental telegraphy and other occult subjects, but in grief burned all the works.

When his other daughter Jean passed only a few years later, Twain wrote his last daughter Clara, describing an unusual experience he had in the room where Jean died. She detailed this experience in her biography, **My Father, Mark Twain.** Her father wrote her that, *"for one who does not believe in spirits, I have had a most peculiar experience".* He explained that as he entered the room where Jean had died, something very odd happened. *"You know how warm it always is in there, and there are no draughts. All at once I felt a cold current of air about me. I thought the door must be open; but it was closed. I said: 'Jean, is this you trying to let me know that you have found the others?' Then the cold air was*

CONNECTICUT
The Mark Twain House & Museum

gone."
— excerpt from her biography, **My Father, Mark Twain**, by Clara Twain

With so many unusual encounters and situations in his past, it's no surprise Twain may have softened his stance regarding ghosts. His own passing in the shadow of Haley's Comet, as he predicted, marked yet another instance of unusual phenomenon in his storied life. Perhaps that's why many believe Twain himself is among the restless spirits found at his old former residence.

The Ghosts of The Mark Twain House and Museum

Reports of paranormal activity connected to the house have been coming in for years. Guests and staff have described encountering shadow figures, unexplained sounds, and disembodied voices or whispering. Especially in areas that are roped off and forbidden to most visitors and employees. A security guard saw a tray fly across the room of its own means, and hit a pipe. Other employees have had the lights turn themselves on, and seen full-bodied apparitions roaming the floors. They've even spotted strange figures in the windows of the building after hours.

Unlike many other haunted hotspots, the museum embraces their "haunts' and even offers ghost tours. On these tours, guides and guests alike have encountered some of the previously mentioned paranormal activity. They've also experienced the disembodied "tugging" of arms, legs, and clothes. This typically in areas where Twain's children played. These witnesses have compared the experience to a child trying to get their attention (especially female visitors and mothers in particular). They've also had watches and bracelets suddenly fall off (sometimes several on different people's arms at the same time).

The ethereal sounds of child like giggling have also been heard by these guests. Along with other strange activity. As they mention on the tours, there are three ghosts in particular that are believed to be the sources for most of this unusual activity.

The first is thought to be Twain's family butler George. He is especially active in his old bedroom, but is encountered throughout the house. He seems to enjoy making loud banging knocks and noises.

The Lady in White

A second spirit, the semi-transparent apparition of a "Lady in White" has been spotted by many, adorned in early period dress and hairstyle. Her ghost reportedly walks through areas of the house before dematerializing. Those who have gotten a closer look at her, claim she bears a resemblance to Twain's daughter Susy. They suggest Susy's ghost might be a "crisis apparition". This was first defined by 19th-century paranormal researchers, as the vision or sense of a loved one around their time of death.

13

CONNECTICUT

Historic Haunts of the North II

Twain's Ghost

'The reports of my death have been greatly exaggerated.'
— Mark Twain

The most famous member of the Clemens family that reportedly manifests in the house is that of Mark Twain himself. While encountered throughout the house, he seems to be discovered most commonly in the Billiards Room, his old "haunt" while working. Many people report smelling cigar smoke, this despite the fact that no smoking is allowed on property. Many believe his spirit may still be lingering in the building, enjoying a cigar. Others have reported heavy tapping sounds as if someone is tapping their fingers on the table, desk, wall, etc. As someone would do while thinking. Maybe Twain is tapping his fingers while working on another story.

The amount of activity reported in the former Twain residence has drawn the attention of several in the paranormal field (like Lorraine Warren, among others). The house has been investigated and featured in numerous paranormal television shows by several ghost hunting groups. Many of these groups have captured EVPs, EMF readings, and other evidence. So much so, that several have visited on multiple occasions and filmed specials here.

My Own Thoughts

My own research into the house has turned up nothing malevolent. I do believe the house may have several haunts, Twain being chief among them. Perhaps he is still here keeping an eye on his house, and possibly working on his next Great American Novel. **The Mark Twain House and Museum** is one of Connecticut's best known attractions, and a great Historic Haunt. I encourage everyone to visit this amazing place to learn more about it and help preserve it. Samuel Longhorne Clemens (Mark Twain) remains an American treasure. A humorist, essayist, and writer, who, thus far is without equal, but who knows, maybe the next time Haley's Comet passes…

CONNECTICUT

THE LEGEND OF SLEEPING GIANT
Blue Hills area, Hamden, Connecticut

Sleeping Giant Photographer Morrowlong Wikipedia Creative Commons

Nestled in the Blue Hills/Mount Carmel region of Connecticut is one of the most unusual locations in America. It's a prominent landscape, a traprock mountain just eight miles north of New Haven that stands 739 feet tall and is visible for miles. This unique mountain, when viewed from the north or the south, has an "anthropomorphic" resemblance to a human figure slumbering. This has earned it the name **Sleeping Giant**. The majority of the mountain is located in the aptly named **Sleeping Giant State Park**. The Giant in Hamden has a long recorded history. It is well known in the area for its rugged topography, distinct human-like "features", clifftop vistas, mythology, and the fact that it's considered by many to be one of the most haunted regions in the state!

Sleeping Giant State Park
Kenneth C. Zirkel
Wikipedia Creative Commons

The Story of The Sleeping Giant

Long before European colonists arrived, the Native Americans of the Quinnipiac Tribes inhabited the area. They would tell their stories of Hobbomock, a wicked and ill-tempered giant. Hobbomock was said to contain the spirit of the souls of the dead. He tended to only do things that pleased him, and threw temper tantrums when things didn't go his way. On one fateful occasion he became so enraged about the mistreatment of his people, that he stomped his feet down in anger. So violent was his reaction, that he diverted the course of the Connecticut River. In doing so, he caused a flood that destroyed many villages and led to much distress among the mortals.

Keihtan, a good spirit, felt pity for the plight of the mortals, and decided Hobbomock needed to be dealt with before he could wreak any more havoc in the future. However, Hobbomock was a divine creature and Keihtan could not kill him. Instead, Keihtan waited for his chance to act. One day, after a particularly large eating binge, the giant grew weary and fell asleep. Seizing his chance,

15

CONNECTICUT
Historic Haunts of the North II

Keihtan cast a spell on him so that he would never awaken again. As time passed, the earth and the trees grew to cover the slumbering behemoth. Peace had been returned to the area, and the mortals had been spared any more outbreaks of the Giant's wrath. He has been said to have been asleep ever since.

Oh yeah, and the Bobcat

Quinnipiac University's Mount Carmel campus lies just at the feet of the Sleeping Giant, At orientation students at the University are told the "Legend of the Bobcat" (the mascot of the school). This story involves Hobbomock's companion, a bobcat. The bobcat was spared from the spell that put the Giant into his eternal sleep under the condition that he now defends the Sleeping Giant and the surrounding area. According to this lore, the bobcat can therefore be seen around campus keeping a watchful eye on the school and the Sleeping Giant. Bobcats were not originally a part of the Quinnipiac legend, but the students of the school have embraced the story and the popular mountain as if they always were.

The Mountain's History

In the mid-19th century New England experienced a surge of interest in the mountain as a retreat from industrialization and urbanization. This resulted in the building of summer cottages on the Sleeping Giant and at other locations along the Metacomet Ridge (an area that extends from Connecticut into Massachusetts). In 1888, a gentleman named John H. Dickerman opened what he called Blue Hills Park after building a pavilion and a carriage road on the Sleeping Giant.

In the early 20th century, Judge Willis Cook, who owned land in Sleeping Giant's first ridge area, leased some of the land to Mount Carmel Traprock Company for quarrying. In the effort of quarrying to create flat and even surfaces and get building materials from it, the shape of Sleeping Giant began to change. Public outrage grew, and the Traprock Company's neighbors and others in the region, began a community effort to preserve the mountain and stop the quarrying. Fundraising began and donations of land followed.

In 1924, the **Sleeping Giant Park Association** (SGPA) was formed. In 1925, **Mt. Carmel State Park** was created after 197 acres were turned over to the State Park and Forest Commission. In 1928, the park's name was switched to **Sleeping Giant**. By 1933, private donations and efforts by a Miss Helen Porter helped raise the approximately $32,000 dollars needed to buy the land from the Traprock Company. This saved the Sleeping Giant's "head", but was no small feat considering it was the middle of the Great Depression.

In 1939, the Work Progress Administration made improvements, including building the Sleeping Giant Tower at the top of the third ridge. In 1960, Norman Griest and Richard Elliot planned out 11 trails encompassing some 30 plus miles and began working on them. In 1986, the Tower was added to the National Register of Historic Places.

CONNECTICUT
Sleeping Giant State Park

Unfortunately, in May of 2018 a tornado, just west of Sleeping Giant State Park transitioned into a half mile wide, seven mile long, 100-mph microburst, that eventually reached the park. This toppled nearly every pine tree in the main picnic area and did extensive damage to the park. To recover, the park closed for a year to allow for cleanup efforts. It reopened to the public in June of 2019 offering its visitors a cleaned up version of Sleeping Giant's human-like features.

Sleeping Giant's Features

The distinct look of a reclining giant is achieved mostly through the mountain's five ridges. The "Giant's" profile and distance features are its "head" at 670 feet high, which is marked by a 400 foot cliff. A second ridge marks the Giant's chest at 710 feet. His left knee and right leg are marked by two ridges each about 700 feet high. Lastly, the stone observation tower located on the Giant's left hip is the highest point at 739 feet.

Sleeping Giant's "head"
Ethan Long
Wikipedia
Creative Commons

Other Unusual Features

Much of the mountain's makeup consists of Basalt, an iron rich volcanic rock. This rock turns reddish or rusty brown in appearance when exposed to the air. This is where the mountain gets its red appearance from (not from a giant red with anger). In addition, the Basalt breaks into octagonal and pentagonal shaped columns. These create a "postpile" appearance (a term for what an area looks like after a pile up of rocks). These columns are clearly visible under the Sleeping Giant ledges.

Sleeping Giant also boasts multiple pine tree forests, which exude a relaxing and pleasant smelling chemical called pinene. The dense foliage in parts of the park give it an almost carpeted appearance. Sleeping Giant also contains areas of unique "microclimates" unusual to New England. Because of this varied terrain, the park contains many state-listed or globally rare species.

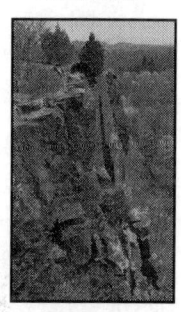

"chin area" and Basalt rock
Wikipedia
Creative Commons

Dead Man's Cave

There is another unusual and well known part of the park that is sometimes difficult to find called "Dead Man's Cave". The cave has existed for a very long time and consists of a series of chambers formed by fallen rocks. On Good Friday in 1873, two boys traveled up the mountain looking for the cave (then called "Abraham's Cave"). The cave was known to be an impressive hollow located on the "left hip" of the Sleeping Giant. While harder to squeeze into at its entrance for all but the smallest of folks, it was reportedly large enough inside to hold a

17

CONNECTICUT
Historic Haunts of the North II

dozen men. Unfortunately, when the boys arrived they found not only the cave, but a dead man! They discovered a badly decomposed corpse whose identity was a mystery. After a time, the dead man was identified as Edward Barnum, nephew to circus legend P.T. Barnum. This connection to a man know for displaying oddities and curiosities is perhaps, a good starting point for discussing some of the more unusual and paranormal activity at Sleeping Giant.

Sleeping Giant's Paranormal Activity

Besides the idea of a ghost manifesting from Dead Man's Cave, and the possibilities of energies stirred up by the damaging microburst; there have been reports of unusually large spiders, strange incidents, and bizarre occurrences and accidents at Sleeping Giant for years (the mountain climbing regions of the park were closed for a time due to some of these accidents). Some of this can be easily dismissed as the natural byproduct of recreational areas and their frequent hikers, horseback riders, cross-country skiers, and the like over sometimes dangerous terrain. However, there have been persistent rumors in the greater area of natural spiritual energy, especially in the heavily wooded areas and neighboring regions (nearby Bruce Museum in Greenwich famously has two vanishing children's ghosts). The majority of these reports of paranormal activity seem to center around the Tower Castle on the "left hip" of the Sleeping Giant.

The Tower Castle

The Tower Castle is the most popular destination in the park and one of the easiest to reach. A crushed stone path leads to this observation tower on top of the Sleeping Giant's left hip. There have been many accounts of otherworldly activity at the peak, inside, and around the Tower Castle itself. These reports describe a strange man dressed all in black who wanders the grounds where the Tower Castle is located. According to these reports, the man looks normal, but bears a white ring around his left arm. Witnesses claim if you attempt to get close to him, he vanishes into thin air.

Tower and path
Craig R.
Wikipedia Creative Commons

Final Thoughts on Sleeping Giant

If there is spiritual energy at work in the park it may be due to the nature of the place itself. Certain types of stone are thought to capture spiritual energies, volcanic rock like Basalt is reportedly one of them. Sleeping Giant is full of this type of rock. There have also been reports of minor earthquakes from local residents, measured on seismographs (the restless Sleeping Giant moving or snoring perhaps). Seismically active regions are known to sometimes be more paranormally active than those that aren't. Especially in the

Tower at summit
StAkAr Karnak
Wikipedia Creative Commons

CONNECTICUT
Sleeping Giant State Park

case of low magnitude earthquakes. Unfortunately, much of the activity in supposed hauntings might be explained away by these quakes (animals acting scared or weird, objects being knocked off their spots or dislodged from walls, etc.) Sleeping Giant, the park and its Tower Castle have definitely experienced earthquakes.

There are many other reasons the Tower in particular could be active. The Depression Era workers who built the Tower invested a lot of their energy into creating it. It seemed like more than just another public work project to them. They reportedly used to signal their nearby homes from the Tower with mirrors. The Foreman of the group, a man named Harry Webb, left his mark on it in more ways than one. There is a spider and web design in one of the Tower's arch windows (a play on his name no doubt). He also brought his Doberman, "Lucky" to the worksite every day. Lucky's likeness is carved into one side of the tower. This has led some to speculate whether Webb's ghost could be the strange apparition seen near the Tower Castle. We may never know.

Regardless, Sleeping Giant offers a lot for the casual visitor, nature lover, or even those curious about the paranormal. Besides the hiking (32 total trails), butterfly gardens, bird watching areas, climbing, snowshoeing, fishing, and horseback riding; the clifftops offer long and scenic views (atmospheric conditions permitting). The Tower Castle itself offers 360 degree views of some of the most picturesque regions nearby including Long Island Sound and New Haven. Sleeping Giant is one of the most unique geographical features I've encountered, and one of Connecticut's most well known Historic Haunts.

Scary view inside Tower courtesy Bob P.a.
Wikipedia Creative Commons

DELAWARE

THE BATTLE OF COOCH'S BRIDGE, AND THE OTHER HEADLESS HORSEMAN
Cooch's Bridge, Newark, Delaware

In Newark, Delaware, on September 3rd of 1777, a battle would take place between British forces and Colonial soldiers. This battle would mark a turning point in the American Revolutionary War, and for our young country as a whole. This hard fought battle for American Independence left an indelible mark on the bridge area where it took place and the property and state it took place in. The sacrifices of these early patriots should not be forgotten, and in the event that they might be, the restless spirits of those who died seem to come back at times to remind us of our history.

Battle of Cooch's Bridge Monument courtesy Kendigger Wikipedia Creative Commons

The Lead Up to The Battle of Cooch's Bridge

As the month of August was drawing to a close in 1777, an advance force of American Light Infantry from several states under the command of Brigadier General William Maxwell were taking their position. They were stationed west of Christina Creek, between Aikentown and nearby Cooch's Bridge. They were buying time for the rest of the American forces. These soldiers were given simple orders, to give the British " as much trouble as you possibly can". They began to engage their enemy on August 30th, two miles south of Cooch's Bridge.

The Americans were greatly outnumbered and outgunned. To counter their obvious disadvantages, they use guerrilla techniques they learned from the Native Americans. While they had some early success with their hit and run tactics; they had been driven back by the advancing British near Iron Side by the beginning of September.

The Battle of Cooch's Bridge

The Battle of Coach's Bridge was fought on September 3rd, 1777. It was unique in many ways, it was the only Revolutionary War battle fought in Delaware. It also marked the first time the "Stars and Stripes" were flown in battle.

The British and Hessian troops were under the command of General Cornwallis, while American forces were under General George Washington. The

DELAWARE
The Battle of Cooch's Bridge

American forces laid an ambush that successfully repelled several British and Hessian charges until their ammunition was depleted. Eventually, the British forces took the Bridge and the surrounding property, burning several buildings in the process. General Cornwallis used the Cooch Family House as his headquarters for the next week as the British regrouped.

During the battle the American forces lost some 30 men. One of these was reportedly a young Colonial Volunteer named Charlie Miller. A British cannonball is said to have decapitated the young soldier, as he rode across the cemetery on his horse during the skirmish. The cannonball continued on, reportedly striking the wall of the Welsh Tract Baptist Church between two larger windows.

Welsh Tract Baptist Church with repaired cannonball damage public domain image

The same forces that killed Charlie Miller would march from the Cooch property to defeat the Colonists in the Battle of Brandywine. General Cornwallis would go on to capture the capital city of Philadelphia before the tides of war would eventually turn. Fortunately for us, the British forces would ultimately surrender to General Washington, and the Battle of Cooch's Bridge would make the history books.

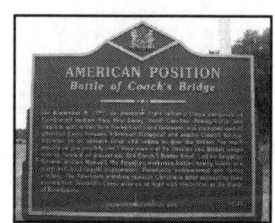

Battle of Cooch's Bridge Roadside Plaque Delaware Public Archives

While the site of the battle has monuments and plaques to identify it, the Cooch Family are working with historical societies and several state groups to restore the site and the surrounding property. Educational programs and guided tours are available for the Bridge site and the Family property. Visitors can learn more of the living history of the place, but they may also learn a bit about the history of the unliving there as well.

Paranormal Accounts of the Area

Many visitors have described a variety of supernatural activity at the site. Among the more common are eerie sounds and ghostly apparitions. According to eyewitnesses, these apparitions often include soldiers roaming the area clad in Revolutionary War era uniforms. These disembodied souls seem to be fighting the battle once again. They are seen engaging in combat while the ethereal sounds of musket fire and bayonets clashing arise. These instances are typically accompanied by distant auditory phenomenon that may include sudden cannon fire, the drumming of a marching military band, and the mournful cries of wounded soldiers. Eyewitnesses have also described a lone soldier's ghost (typically seen at dusk or during early morning hours), that is seen, transparent, but still standing

DELAWARE

guard at the bridge. The most disturbing of these phantom encounters, however, seems to be attached to the Headless Horseman.

Headless Horseman
Author's Collection

The Other Headless Horseman

Many of us are familiar with Washington Irving's Headless Horseman, the Hessian soldier from his " Legend of Sleep Hollow" tale (check out the Sleepy Hollow Cemetery story later in this book). But Irving's Horseman is apparently not the only one. Another Headless Horseman, believed to be the spirit of Charlie Miller, has been encountered here. Delaware's Headless Horseman is often spotted riding a spectral horse accompanied by bugle sounds and the sounds of thundering disembodied hooves. If reports are to be believed, he has been seen searching for his head along the I-95 median, tollbooth lanes, and wooded sections of Welsh Tract Road. He seems to appear more often on the anniversary of the Battle of Cooch's Bridge.

Final Thoughts

There seems to be an abundance of paranormal activity at this site (like many famous battlegrounds). So much so that it has attracted numerous investigative and ghost hunting groups. These groups often claim to have captured EMF spikes, EVPs, and unusual cold spots. I encourage fans of the paranormal and history buffs to check out this Historic Haunt and really get into it. Just be sure you don't lose your head.

DELAWARE

THE PARANORMAL PEA PATCH
Fort Delaware, Pea Patch Island, Delaware

There's a legend in the Delaware River area that claims hundreds of years ago a shoal in the River caused a ship carrying peas to run aground. Some of the peas dropped off the ship, germinated in the shoal, and Pea Patch Island was born. The Islands' prime defensive location for protecting Wilmington and Philadelphia helped draw the attention of early American military forces. They constructed fortifications to help guard the region. Today the Fort that stands on the island, and its checkered past draw fans of history, while its haunted residents draw the attention of ghost hunters and fans of the paranormal.

Fort Delaware today by Brendan Mackie Wikipedia Creative Commons

The Founding of Fort Delaware

During the War of 1812 a seawall and dikes were built around the island of Pea Patch to help fortify it. In 1813, recognition of the area's defensive value led the state to deed the islands to the federal government. In December 1817, construction began on a star shaped fort under the supervision of Capt. Samuel Babcock (1819 – 1824), who had previously fortified the area during the war.

Public Domain image showing seawall

The Fort was completed, but only after years of delays from the proposed date. The delays were mostly due to the uneven settling of the structure, the marshy nature of the island, and other unforeseen situations. Despite these reasonable explanations, the delays almost led to Babcock's court martial.

The first documented commander was Maj. Alexander C. W. Fanning who took command shortly before 1825. Around 1829 command would pass to Maj. Benjamin Kendrick Pierce (older brother to our 14th President, Franklin Pierce). In February of 1831, the U.S. Army Corps of Engineers sent a Lieut. Stephen Tuttle to find possible solutions to the Fort's foundation issue. Later that month a fire broke out in Lieut. Tuttles quarters. The fire destroyed much of the improvement

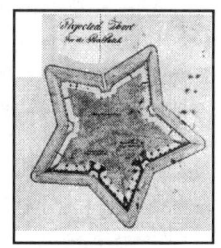
Fort Drawing U.S. Army Corps of Engineers Public Domain

23

DELAWARE
Historic Haunts of the North II

work and large parts of the fort. It was no surprise then in 1833 when Fort Delaware was torn down due to the damage and room was made for a new fortification. The rubble from the demolished star shaped fort served to reinforce the seawall around the island.

A Capt. Delafield would design the second version of the fort, described as "a huge bastioned polygonal form". Work continued through the late 1850s. (it wasn't declared finished until 1868). During the Civil War, (while it was still under construction), after legal delays, extensive excavation work, and the complicated process of driving timbers into the island's soft mud, the decision was made to use the fort as a prison and a prisoner of war camp. It was used to house captured Confederate soldiers, convicted Federal soldiers, and political prisoners and privateers.

Fort Delaware Civil War era Public Domain image

Fort Delaware's Hardships

The Fort's design envisioned accommodating several thousand men. Unfortunately, during its service as a prison the fort would grow to house some 33,000 men. Of these about 2,500 prisoners died from contracting typhoid, malaria, diarrhea, scurvy, pneumonia, and from a smallpox epidemic that broke out in 1863. In addition, some prisoners and guards froze to death and others died trying to escape. In fact, approximately 273 escapes were documented. Many of these attempts included hiding in coffins, bribing guards, and jumping through bathroom holes into the river to try to get past the escape deterrents (guards, strong river currents, sharks, and other hazards).

In 1878, after the Civil War a hurricane hit and caused great damage. In 1885 a tornado struck and did even more. The fort, even in its damaged state was "on call" during the Spanish-American War, World War I, and World War II, being part of the coastal defense network.

In 1947 after being declared a "surplus site" it was acquired from the U.S. government by the state of Delaware. It became a state park, encompassing all of Pea Patch Island. In 1971 it was listed on the National Register of Historic Places. In 2009, Delaware indirectly recognized its status as a haunted historic site by working with an area non-profit paranormal investigations group to create a variety of paranormal tours and investigations for the public. It is now a Museum and apparent home to several spirits.

Paranormal Experiences on the Tour and at the Fort

A group on tour was listening to a tour guide in costume describing details of the Fort's past. Because of this they weren't surprised when they saw a

DELAWARE
Fort Delaware

woman appear in an old style dress. In fact, the group thought she was part of the tour until they saw her walk right through a wall!

The apparitions of Civil War soldiers have been encountered and reported that disappear mere moments after they appeared. Some apparitions have even been caught on camera at the fort. Ghostly gunshots have been known to startle the guests and the sounds of shouts and screams have done the same.

Many of the Forts' resident haunts are known to the tour guides and visitors from records and other historic evidence. Some twelve Confederate generals spent time as prisoners at Fort Delaware. Among these officers was General James Jay Archer, whose bearded spirit has been spotted numerous times, clad in gray in the area where he was incarcerated. A Union Army volunteer, an Italian immigrant named Private Stefano, slipped and fell at the fort during the war. He hit his head and broke his neck on the floor. His spirit is often encountered in the area where he met his demise. In addition to these apparitions, a multitude of other unusual activity and manifestations are common on the fort grounds.

Frightening disembodied voices, rattling chains, and moans and screams are heard frequently near the old dungeon. Violent screams and cries for help are reported on the upper floors, and ethereal music and children's disembodied laughter are encountered in other areas. Mysterious lights have been seen on the fort (even while closed and devoid of people and power), as well as a plethora of reports of orb activity.

So frequent are the reports of activity in the prisoner's barracks, mess hall, officer's kitchen, officer's quarters, ordinance room areas, dungeon and west area of the Fort, that it has drawn national and international attention. Famed ghost hunting groups have filmed and investigated here on several occasions. They also encountered unusual noises and sounds, and recorded EVPs (electronic voice phenomenon), which reportedly included ethereal conversations, screams, and at least a few instances and situations in which investigators were "growled at". The spirits in these situations were even reported to go further, actually pushing or shoving some of the investigators!

Pea Patch Island is an intriguing site and an apparent hotbed of otherworldly activity. It is a definite stop if you are on the hunt for the paranormal. Chances are pretty good that you will experience something from the other side at Fort Delaware State Park. It's no wonder with its rich historic past and series of unfortunate deaths, that the living might be drawn to encounter the spirits of the deceased at this Historic Haunt.

MAINE

HITCHHIKERS, HEALING WATERS, AND HAUNTED ACTIVITY AT THE POLAND SPRINGS INN
Poland Springs Inn, Poland, Maine

Maine has no shortage of historic and interesting places. While I haven't visited as much of the state as I'd like, there are several stories and places that have captured my attention. Less than an hour from the popular coastal town of Portland, Maine lies the city of Poland. This town is a great spot to visit with great places to experience and great stories. One of the more interesting and unique is the story of the haunted Poland Springs Inn.

Poland Springs Resort courtesy of Wikipedia Creative Commons and photographer Magicpiano

A History of Healing Waters and Hosting

The late seventeenth century is when many believe the story of Poland Springs begins. However, long before Europeans occupied the land, there were stories of the local springs and its healing properties. In fact, there are stories about Molly Ockett, a skilled healer and Abenaki woman. The Abenaki were an indigenous people of the Northeastern woodlands of Canada and the United States. Molly had a reputation as a healer among her tribe and early Colonial Americans. Her healing efforts often involved the local waters and their vaunted healing powers. In fact, she was reputed to have saved the life of Hannibal Hamlin, future Vice President of the U.S.

Well before the time of Hannibal Hamlin and Molly Ockett, Jabez Ricker and his family moved to Poland (then called Parkerstown) from Alfred, Maine. Not long after their arrival travelers knocked on their door looking for a place to stay. Sensing an opportunity, the family began operating an Inn and farm on the property. By 1797 they opened a brand new building, the Wentworth Ricker Inn.

Jabez passed in 1827. His son Wentworth continued the family business. Unfortunately, Wentworth would fall ill and be diagnosed with a rare and

MAINE
The Poland Springs Inn

fatal kidney disorder. Trusting his fate to the healing power of the local waters; Wentworth was not only cured, he became healthy and vigorous again! He even built the road that runs through the resort himself. The story of Wentworth's recovery only increased the belief in the local water's recuperative properties.

In 1844, Wentworth's son, Hiram Ricker, having medical issues of his own, reportedly drank only water from the edge of the property and was cured of his malady. The Ricker family began sharing the water in 1845. By 1859, Hiram Ricker — convinced the water from the spring possessed curative properties — started bottling and selling the water.

As they started selling the water, the Ricker family also began to promote the health benefits of the healing waters on the sight. The enterprising family positioned their property as a retreat, a country getaway with things to do where the well-to-do could get well and have fun in the process. The popularity of the place and number of patrons quickly skyrocketed.

Plans to Grow Spring to Life

The property became one of the biggest draws in the country and a place where you would find America's political and social elite gather. To accommodate this influx of visitors, Hiram Ricker expanded the property with the addition of the 100 room Poland Springs House in 1876. Still, it wasn't enough!

So again, Poland Springs resort underwent another expansion. This time far more extensive. The property grew to over 350 guest rooms. Besides the rooms, Poland Springs resort would add a pool room, barbershop, photography studio, dance studio, music hall, and dining facilities to seat 500 guests! It also boasted the new and rare innovations of elevators and fire sprinkler systems.

Focused as they were at the time with the most up to date means to house and provide amenities to their visitors, the Ricker family took note of their state's entry into the Columbia Exposition. The Columbia Exposition of the **Chicago World's Fair of 1893** featured new and creative building concepts from across the country, including the Maine State Building (Maine's official entry into the event). The Rickers were impressed by this building, as were the many visitors to the world's fair. To further enlarge the site, the Rickers purchased the building from the State and had it disassembled and shipped in sixteen freight cars to the Poland Springs Resort to be reassembled and used on property.

The family's fortunes and that of Poland Springs continued to grow. In 1896 an 18 hole golf course was added, one of the first in the state. A new springhouse and bottling plant were opened in 1907. The Presidential Inn was

MAINE
Historic Haunts of the North II

added in 1913, appropriate perhaps, since the property would be visited by Presidents, celebrities, and even sports stars like Babe Ruth.

The Family's Fortunes Turn for the Worse and the Property Changes Hands

Even the healing waters on the property couldn't cure the problems the 1930s brought to the family. The Great Depression and its aftermath saw the family's control over their empire disappear. The businesses were bought and sold several times during the ensuing years.

In 1962 Saul Feldman purchased the water compa-

Poland Spring and Water ad circa 1919 image is in the public domain

ny and the resort. He also built the Maine Inn on the grounds. Saul tried to bring more attention, new clientele and new direction to the site. For a time it worked. Saul hosted Joan Crawford and the **Route 66** TV film crew, Boxer Sonny Liston (while he trained for his fight with Cassius Clay), and even broadcaster Jack Parr. However, the resurgence wouldn't last.

By 1966 Saul began leasing the property, including leasing the grounds and buildings (including the Poland Springs House) to the U.S. Government for the Job Corps program. This government group stayed until 1969. The Maharishi of India leased the property in 1970 and the Poland Springs was closed. By 1971 past lessees had rendered most of the buildings uninhabitable.

In 1972 Mel Robbins, a developer, came to Poland Springs to tear down the hotels and build. Instead, the historic property spoke to him and he saw great potential. He worked tirelessly over the next several years to save the property from demolition and turn it around.

He met and married his wife Cyndi (in her youth a waitress at the Inn at Poland Springs) and the two continued to work to bring the property back to

The Poland Springs Inn

its glory days. Unfortunately, in 1975 a tragedy struck. A fire on July 3rd of that year would see the Poland Springs House burnt to the ground! The couple shifted gears and worked to rebuild and renew their shared dream for the property's prosperity until Mel's passing in 2007. Today Cyndi and family are keeping Mel's vision alive.

The Paranormal Poland Springs

Visitors to the Poland Springs Inn may view Mel Robbin's vision for themselves, but it may not be the only vision they encounter. Guests and employees claim to have seen the apparition of Hiram Ricker who supposedly haunts the property (especially the Presidential Inn) and the springs. Those witnesses have identified Ricker's ghost, claiming he looked exactly like the photos the inn has on display. A disembodied male voice is often heard in the lobby and in empty rooms along with footsteps, especially in the early morning hours. The staff seems to attribute this phenomenon to Ricker's ghost as well. Many claim Ricker's spirit is mischievous and likes to play tricks. Among these tricks, most often, is objects which are moved to very unusual places.

Ricker's ghost is not the only one encountered on site. The spirit of an unidentified woman has also crossed paths with guests and employees. In fact, there are certain parts of the property employees will not dare to venture into because of their fear of encountering her! However, she's not the only female spirit active in the area.

The Haunted Hitchhikers

The road leading to the Poland Springs property (Route 26) has at least two examples of other female phantoms. While they are different in dress and appearance, both have appeared in similar ways and with similar requests. They both apparently need a lift.

The first is a woman in a wedding dress. Her identity has not been discovered. However, this bride was reported to have been struck and killed in route to her wedding!

The second is encountered in a faded prom dress. The style of the dress suggests quite a bit of time has passed. Like the bride, she is thought to also be a victim of an unfortunate event that kept her from her destination.

In both cases, these mysterious maidens are encountered on the side of the road entreating drivers to stop and give them a ride. In many cases they appear to be intelligent haunts holding interactive conversations with their benefactors to varying degrees. In most accounts both vanish just before entering the vehicle or shortly thereafter, sometimes disappearing after the drivers have begun to take them where they wished to go.

MAINE
Historic Haunts of the North II

My Visit to the Property and Parting Thoughts

Some believe the natural springs possess an energy that the spirits can feed off of, drawing the vitality needed to manifest themselves. Water is a known conductor of energy. In my experiences running Historic Haunts Investigations, we have encountered much more paranormal activity when near springs, lakes, rivers, and the ocean. This might help explain the frequent reports of apparitions in and around the property and the springs.

My tour of the resort was way too quick, but I couldn't help but notice how beautiful it was. It also stood out to me as a great example in the north of an often reported paranormal encounter, that of the hitchhiking woman. This is one of the most common instances of paranormal activity reported across the country and one that inevitably achieves legendary status in those regions.

The state of Maine has a mystical quality during the summer that tends to draw many tourists. Even among the other state sights, the Poland Springs Inn is one of the more magical destinations. The property boasts three Inns, multiple excellent restaurants, a golf course, and rich history. The Poland Springs Inn is one of my favorite Historic Haunts in the Pine Tree State. I highly encourage my readers to visit this beautiful property for themselves. If you see a strange woman on the side of the road on the way there, don't be surprised if she asks for a ride!

MARYLAND

JOHN WILKES BOOTH AND THE GHOST WHOSE NAME IS MUDD
Dr. Samuel Mudd's House, Waldorf, Maryland

I'm a big fan of history, and one of the most impactful days in America History was April 14, 1865, the day John Wilkes Booth shot President Abraham Lincoln. The President would pass in the early hours of the April 15th. This killing would forever alter our collective conscience and set in motion one of the biggest manhunts ever for the people involved. One of the men involved in these events was Dr, Samuel Mudd. We may never know whether Mudd was simply a caring doctor or co-conspirator. However, the ghosts of the past do seem to be on display at Dr, Mudd's House in Waldorf, Maryland.

Dr. Samuel Mudd House Preservation Maryland courtesy Wikipedia Creative Commons

Dr, Samuel Mudd's History

Samuel Alexander Mudd was born in December of 1833. He grew up on his father's tobacco plantation (Oak Hill), which was worked by slaves. He studied medicine at the **University of Maryland**, Baltimore. He came back to Charles County to practice medicine and married his childhood sweetheart in 1857.

Mudd's father gave him farm land and a house as a wedding gift. Dr. Mudd's home was built between 1857 and 1859. Mudd had slaves himself to help on the tobacco farm. Maryland abolished slavery in 1864. Without his slaves to help with the farm, Mudd considered selling it. It was during that year that he was reportedly introduced to someone interested in purchasing it, 26 year old actor John Wilkes Booth.

Dr. Samuel Mudd Public Domain

The Fateful Day, What is Known

On April 14th, 1865 John Wilkes Booth went into Ford's Theatre and shot President Lincoln in his private box during a play. He jumped to the stage for a dramatic escape, but not before he broke his leg when he landed. He rode from the theatre on horseback with an accomplice David Herold, and fled Washington.

MARYLAND
Historic Haunts of the North II

(for more details, check out my story about Ford's Theatre in ***Historic Haunts of the North***). Booth and his accomplice arrived at Dr. Mudd's house at 4 a.m. on April 15, 1865. Mudd cut Booth's boot off his injured leg, and set it by splintering it. He also gave him a shoe to wear. Mudd arranged for a carpenter to make a crutch. John Wilkes Booth paid Dr. Mudd $25 for his service.

Booth and his accomplice Herold, slept in the first bedroom of Mudd's house on the second floor. They stayed at the house and farm for some 12 to 15 hours. Mudd traveled to Bryantown on April 15th for errands. There he reportedly learned of Lincoln's assassination. He returned home.

Where the "Potential Plot" Thickens

It is uncertain whether Booth and his compatriot were gone by the time Mudd returned, if he met them along the way, or urged them to leave when he returned. Mudd waited to notify the authorities, claiming he didn't want to be leave his family alone in case the assassins returned. Eventually, the authorities reached Mudd's home and questioned him. They discovered the bed Booth slept in and did a quick search before continuing on.

For some reason, Mudd sent the authorities in the opposite direction when asked what direction Booth had gone. Mudd's story began to exhibit some inconsistencies. The authorities returned to the Mudd house at which time Mudd had his wife turn over Booth's boot (which had been hidden in the attic). Authorities also found more evidence during the second search. Mudd was arrested and set to stand trial with the other "conspirators".

The Trial

During the trial, Mudd's defense team tried to portray him as a Union supporter, and doctor who was just doing his job to help heal a patient. He claimed he'd never met Booth or the other conspirators. However, Mudd's story changed under interrogation. His former slaves testified that they heard him say on several occasions that President Lincoln should be shot. It also was discovered that Mudd had been seen in the company of some of the conspirators one year before. A written statement from one of the other conspirators also claimed that Booth had sent liquor and provisions two weeks before to Mudd's farm.

Dr. Mudd was found guilty of aiding and conspiring in the murder of the President. He was sentenced to life in prison at Fort Jefferson in the Dry Tortugas, off the coast of Key West Florida.

What Happened at Fort Jefferson

Mudd was imprisoned at the Fort along with a few of his coconspirators. In September of 1865, Mudd apparently tried to escape and failed. He had his privileges revoked and was put in much less comfortable accommodations.

MARYLAND
Dr. Samuel Mudd House

During the fall of 1867, Yellow Fever broke out at the fort and the doctor on duty there died. Dr. Mudd agreed to take care of the patients and do whatever he could to help. Because of his actions, President Andrew Johnson pardoned him in 1869.

Fort Jefferson
National Park Service
Public Domain

After the Pardon

Mudd's friends and family welcomed him back and showed great support. Dr. Mudd later died in 1883 at the age of 49 years old of pneumonia. Mudd was buried at St. Mary's Catholic Church (where he once supposedly met Booth to talk about selling the farm). It is said Mudd's spirit might still be found in his home.

The Ghosts of the Mudd House

Mudd's house has been described by witnesses as haunted. Many people have detailed accounts of a strange light that has been seen going through the rooms and along the property for years, even when the place is empty. Many neighbors reported these lights during the 20th century. Other witnesses have reported heavy footfalls, like the sound of old style boots being heard, and low voices and disembodied conversations taking place.

The most common reports of paranormal activity in the house seem to involve John Wilkes Booth and Mudd himself. The front bedroom upstairs is called the "Booth Room". Legends claim no matter how tightly the bed's sheet and covers are in the evening, a distinct human impression can be seen in the bed by morning (even though the room has no occupants). Many have speculated this could be the spirit of John Wilkes Booth.

Dr. Mudd's spirit is also encountered at the house. In fact, it is said it was his spirit that "compelled" his granddaughter to turn the place into a museum. His apparition has reportedly been seen wearing a cap and a long brown topcoat.

Some Interesting Details and Final Thoughts

Mudd's family has been trying for years to get his record expunged. They claim that he is completely innocent. However, there are a few details that would seem to call this into question. The obvious ones being why hide the evidence (unless you're worried you've been pulled into something inadvertently), but harder to explain, why send the military in the wrong direction. But there are others, for example, it is strange that he was discovered to have met up with Booth more than he accounted for and kept that fact secret. Further, for someone who claimed he had nothing to do with the plot and the conspirators, he allowed Edmund Spangler, another pardoned conspirator to move to his farm in 1873. Spangler

MARYLAND
Historic Haunts of the North II

was welcomed by the family. Spangler lived there until he passed some 18 months later. There are many who speculate that Mudd may have been on board for the original plan, the kidnapping of the President (which the earlier meetings with Booth would help explain), but not as willing to go along with the President's murder.

    Whether you believe Mudd or not this story and its aftermath, are a part of American History. The actions of these men leave an indelible mark as pronounced as the "paranormal" outlines of Booth's ghost upstairs. This is one very important Historic Haunt.

MARYLAND

THE MYSTERIOUS MIDDLETON TAVERN

Middleton Tavern, Annapolis, Maryland

I'm definitely a sucker for tales connected to the early history of the United States and our Founding Fathers. There are plenty of these tales connected to the original colonies. One of the more intriguing lies one block from the US Naval Academy in downtown Annapolis, Maryland. This Georgian style building began as a private residence, occupied around 1740 by Elizabeth Bennet and sold in 1750 to Horatio Middleton. I'm speaking of course of the reportedly haunted Middleton Tavern.

Middleton Tavern postcard from author's collection

The Tavern's History

Middleton bought the building from Bennett, because by law he needed to have lodgings for his customers. He opened Middleton Tavern as an "Inn for seafaring men". Middleton originally called it "Old Inn" where it was known as a tavern selling dry goods. He also owned the ferry company that linked Annapolis to the Eastern Shore of the Chesapeake Bay. The site also served as a ship's Carpenter's yard. No surprise since Middleton's ferry was popular because it significantly shortened the travel time from Philadelphia to Virginia. Middleton himself was the Virginia delegate to the Continental Congress. The tavern became popular with members of the State House and members of the Continental Congress.

After Middleton's death, his widow Anne operated the tavern. Later the Middleton's son Samuel took over the tavern and the ferry business. Many travelers crossing the bay stopped here. Even George Washington and Benjamin Franklin found their way to the tavern. It has been recorded that Thomas Jefferson gave passage faire to Samuel Middleton to travel to Rock Fall on the Eastern Shore.

Middleton Tavern was more than a tavern. It was described as an early show place of Annapolis with its beautiful garden. During the Revolutionary War, George Mann operated the tavern. Both the tavern and the ferry business

35

MARYLAND
Historic Haunts of the North II

played a supporting role in the troubles of the time. The ferry carried Tench Tilgman on his way to deliver news of Cornwallis' surrender in 1781.

After the Revolutionary War, Samuel Middleton's son, Gilbert operated the tavern. The Middletons sold the property in 1792 to John Randall. Randall would become mayor of Annapolis, and greeted President Monroe during his visit and stay May 28th through 30th, 1818. The tavern would stay in the Randall family until 1854.

In 1864, the property was purchased by Frederick Marx, and it became the Marx Hotel. Marx would operate the hotel during the Civil War years. Marx sold the hotel in 1867 to William Myers, who in turn rented it to a man killed in 1875 by one of his disgruntled employees. The site would play host to a general store and meat market before becoming Tyding's Bar in the early 1900s. The Mandris family came into possession of the building around 1933 They operated a restaurant, soda counter, and souvenir shop there.

Jerry Hardesty bought the building in 1968 from the Mandris, restored the building inside and out and changed the name back to Middleton Tavern. Since then, the building was gutted by fire in 1970 and 73, only to be rebuilt. In 1983. Middletown tavern, underwent extensive remodeling and expansion. A new tavern and oyster bar were added, and the upstairs dining rooms were expanded and decorated to accommodate private parties, meetings, and crowds of hungry diners. Since then, the place has become a popular draw, known statewide. With a beautiful building, great food, and great drinks, it's no wonder some of the past patrons or owners might still be here "in spirit". I know I would be.

Middleton's Mischievous Spirits

The tavern has reportedly experienced paranormal activity for quite some time, and with great frequency. There have been numerous reports of unexplained voices, disembodied footsteps, and chairs that pull out by themselves after being pushed in. That's just the tip of the iceberg.

The staff claimed that an entity named Roland makes his presence known often in first floor dining rooms. Roland often appears as a man clothed in Revolutionary War era garments staring out a window at the harbor. People who have witnessed him say he seems to be watching for something, maybe even a ship, since he is gazing out at the harbor. His presence is often accompanied by cigar smoke (a stand out in a non-smoking building). His ghost has even been seen through the window by people outside the tavern.

Another ghost present at the tavern has at times been thought to be a poltergeist or the spirit of a cook that used to work there. Employees believe it is a male spirit, but no one seems to know who it is. This spirit seems to be a bit mischievous. Plates have been known to just fall off the shelves, glasses fall from the bar walls, and tables with dirty dishes have tipped over on their own. Much of this activity has been witnessed by patrons and employees alike. The spirit has also been known to "steal" drinks, and mess with the beer taps. Witnesses claim that usually, if you ask the spirit to stop, it will.

Shadow Figures

Shadows have often been seen in different locations throughout the tavern, even in locations where there is no apparent way for a shadow to be cast. No one has ever been hurt by them. The shadow figures are known to break dishes and turn the tap lanterns mounted on the walls in the restaurant upside down to get attention. They've also been known to move tables and chairs perhaps for a spectral get together.

The ghostly get togethers are not limited to the tavern's open hours. People have also reported ghostly gatherings going on inside the tavern after hours, when the doors are all locked up tight and the lights are out. During these times passers-bye have heard the sounds of loud conversations and laughter coming from inside the building. They have also reported a flicker of candle light inside the building when the place is closed. I suppose even a ghostly gathering, may need a little light. If you try to approach the doors or windows while this spectral activity is occurring to see or hear what is going on, it abruptly stops.

That's not the only paranormal activity found by witnesses outside of the tavern. In the late 1700s, nearby Franklin Street was the site where Alexander Hastings was reportedly jumped, robbed, and beaten to death. Witnesses claim to have encountered a man running through the alley yelling for help only to be dragged away by what many described as shadow people. These witnesses have even called the police for help. When they arrive and investigate all they find is an empty alley.

Parting Thoughts

The Middleton Tavern is one of the oldest continuosly operating taverns in the United States. It's also a wonderful place to spend an evening, popular inside and outside with the living and apparently the nonliving. This site has been the subject of several podcasts, articles, and it is referenced among Maryland's most haunted locations and taverns. To locals and visitors it's a precious place to enjoy, to us it's a real gem in the Historic Haunts collection.

MASSACHUSETTS

THE SPIRITS OF THE JOSHUA WARD HOUSE

Joshua Ward House, Salem, Massachusetts

I have always felt connected to Salem, Massachusetts. Being a descendent of witches who went through the witch trials, I am keenly aware of this infamous time in the region's history. I'm also familiar with the major historical figures responsible, one of whom resided at 148 Washington Street, the site of the current Joshua Ward House. If paranormal reports are to be believed this resident spirit is still there.

The Joshua Ward House courtesy of Swampyank Wikipedia Creative Commons

The History of the Joshua Ward House

Joshua Ward who was a retired sea captain/merchant built his "mansion" in the mid-1780s. The house was built on the site where the infamous Sheriff George Corwin's house and jail once stood. Sheriff Corwin was nick named "The Strangler" because of his interrogation process used on those suspected of being of witches and warlocks. He carried out many painful death sentences during the Salem Witch Hysteria in 1692 and 1693. Nineteen men and women were executed under his watch and he imprisoned over 160.

Corwin was related to two local judges and connected by marriage to a third. Perhaps that's why he felt free and secure to indulge his more sadistic urges. Besides the strangling that earned him his nickname, he was known to tie victims neck's to their ankles until blood came out their noses. He engaged in other tortures techniques as well. If that wasn't enough, his position of sheriff allowed him to confiscate items and goods from the condemned. This practice he embraced wholeheartedly.

One of Sheriff Corwin's early victims was an old man named Giles Corey. After early torture failed to get Corey to confess to being a warlock, the sheriff moved on to something more brutal. Corey was subjected to an archaic technique in which heavy stones are placed on planks across the body to force a confession. Ever defiant and secure in his innocence instead of confessing Corey looked up at the sheriff and said, "More stones!" During his torture, the old man's tongue lolled out of his mouth and the sheriff callously pushed it back in with his walking stick. The old man was eventually crushed

MASSACHUSSETS
The Spirits of the Joshua Ward House

to death by the weight of the stones, but not before spitting out a curse on all of Salem and its sheriffs in particular.

Sheriff Corwin also accused a wealthy local named Philip English of witchcraft. Unlike the other unfortunates who were accused, English's money allowed him to flee to New York until the hysteria of the witch hunts ended. The sheriff was happy to confiscate his possessions and valuables. When English returned he sued for the return of his property in lengthy court cases that went on for years. Unfortunately for English, the curse Giles Corey placed on the sheriff may have worked. The sheriff died of what has been called a sudden heart attack or mysterious blood ailment in 1697. The court cases remained unresolved. English threatened to steal the corpse and hold it for ransom.

"Arresting a Witch"
by Howard Pyle
Harper's New Monthly Magazine
image is in the public domain

Sheriff Corwin was buried in the basement of the house. Some speculate it was out of fear of English's threat or because the family thought the outraged citizens of Salem would desecrate the grave. His body remained here for many years before it was removed and relocated to the Broad Street Cemetery.

At some point after Corwin's death the house was demolished leaving room for the Joshua Ward House to be built. During the 19th century, it became an upscale hotel called The Washington. It may have been named Washington in honor of George Washington, who visited here in 1789, and requested to stay at the hotel. The Joshua Ward House would also serve as a tavern, book company, and realtor's office before returning once again to a hotel. However, it would seem the living are not the only guests here.

Ghosts in the House

Some of Corwin's victims are known to haunt the Joshua Ward House. Do you blame them? Many are probably still seeking justice for being wrongly accused and executed. The main ghost who seems to haunt this old house is Giles Corey. Corey's apparition has been frequently reported and connected to a variety of paranormal activity. This activity includes; trash cans knocked over by ghostly means, books pulled down from shelves, cold spots, and candles which were never lit found in a puddle of wax.

The spirit of Sheriff Corwin himself has also been seen on the grounds. His ghost is associated with paranormal reports of burning scratches on the arms

39

MASSACHUSETTS
Historic Haunts of the North II

and backs of visitors to the house. Others coming to the house have reported feeling as if they were being strangled by phantom hands. Perhaps this is "the strangler" up to his old tricks. Many people have reported seeing Sheriff Corwin and Giles Corey on the property.

In addition to Sheriff Corwin and Giles Corey's ghostly activity, there has been other paranormal activity reported. Cold spots are often felt throughout the building and other strange occurrences happen on a frequent basis. Brand new candles will be put into the candle holders and will be discovered later on the floor in the shape of an "S". There have also been reports of papers strewn across rooms and dead bolt locks opening themselves.

The Infamous Picture of the Witch

During its tenure as a realtor's office something would happen at the Joshua Ward House that would further draw attention to its haunted reputation. One of the real estate agents was taking Polaroids of her fellow realtors by the entrance for use in listing the place. When the picture was developed it seemed the realtor's face and body were gone and in its place was the image of a black haired "witch". The realtors who had frequently reported paranormal activity in the house thought they had captured a photo of one of the resident spirits. The picture was shared and made news.

Skeptics question the photo claiming the picture merely resembled a woman with a Christmas wreath behind her (I tend to agree). Interestingly enough, since the photo surfaced there have been numerous reports of the witch's ghost seen throughout the building, even by those unfamiliar with the photo and its history. These later reports claim her spirit has been encountered roaming through the hallways of the building, and floating up and down the stairs.

Final Thoughts

I'm glad I didn't get the opportunity to go inside the house when I was in Salem. Sheriff Corwin's ghost might have picked up on the fact that I'm related to a Salem Witch he once convicted. Whether you experience Giles Corey, Sheriff Corwin or the black witch upon your visit to Salem and the Joshua Ward House, it is a must see location in America's historic past and on your Historic Haunts journey.

SEAFOOD AND SEE GHOSTS AT OLD YARMOUTH INN

Old Yarmouth Inn, Restaurant and Tavern, Yarmouth, Massachusetts

The Old Yarmouth Inn was established in 1696 and is the oldest inn on Cape Cod. It was built for the weary traveler located as it was, about halfway from Plymouth to Provincetown (a day and half coach ride each way). Situated on the historic Old King's Highway, it has draw many visitors over its long history. Due to a fire at Town Hall many years ago, there is little documentation on the Inn's history, but the guest registry from the 1860s survives to this day.

Without the documentation it's hard to prove, but the Old Yarmouth Inn has reportedly been used as a dentist office, family homes, a boarding house, and was suggested to have housed Revolutionary War era soldiers. Today, this white two story colonial style structure boasts a basement, attic, three distinct dining rooms (the red room, music room, and main dining room), and a tavern. It also boasts the best homemade classics in seafood on Cape Cod and more than its fair share of ghost stories.

Old Yarmouth Spirits

Most of the reports of paranormal activity at the inn suggest the presence of a male and female ghost. However, fairly recently it is believed that other spirits may have taken up residence, including at least one that apparently considers itself part of the management team. This spirit has been encountered acting up against anyone who acts in a manner unbecoming.

At least some of the spirits thought to exist here are reported to have a sense of humor and some are described as pranksters. Things have been known to disappear then reappear in the strangest places. The spirits here also do not like to be mocked.

Twice, theatrical séances were held and both times little things happened which seemed to show disapproval from the spirit world. During the first séance, some vases in the Red Room's more formal private dining area were found broken perfectly in half. The second time, marbles were found all over the floor, and roses from a vase were found fanned out.

The male ghost originally thought to be occupying the inn was a Mr. Powell, grandfather to a curious little girl named Althea. Althea Powell's grandfather ran his dentist office from the first floor of the Old Yarmouth years ago and many believe that he may still be here. His apparition is said to have surprised at least one guest in the Quisset Harbor Room by asking them why they were in his bed before fading away in front of them. The Powell's granddaughter is connected to the other ghost stories at the Inn as well. One

MASSACHUSSETS
Historic Haunts of the North II

time while Althea was alive and at the Inn she found a secret door in the attic which is believed to be where they housed slaves during the Underground Railroad Era. Some people suggest that a few spirits of the slaves may be lingering here as well.

Another frequent report discusses a female apparition who is believed to have died in her sleep when a fire broke out upstairs. She was rumored to be the mistress of the innkeeper so maybe her death wasn't an accident. Other reports attribute the female apparition to a slave from the Civil War days. Another guest of the inn, and one who is very afraid of ghosts, described seeing the woman and receiving an ethereal foot rub before unseen hands seemed to grab the bed posts and shake and rattle the bed, until the patron flew out of the room and to the porch. A story which seemed to later be confirmed when the innkeeper's 89 year old mother made the claim the next morning that she couldn't sleep due to all the banging and racket across the hall.

A male apparition has also been seen wearing 19th-century clothing with puffy sleeves. He is seen walking throughout the Inn. He maybe the same gentleman ghost whose apparition has been repeatedly spied in the Red Room waiting at his table only to disappear when servers came over to take his order.

Tavern and Elsewhere

Old Yarmouth's Tavern has been the focal point of much paranormal activity. It is here that employees and guests have encountered ash trays that have hovered in the air before slipping and sliding down the bar. The tavern's kitchen equipment has been know to turn itself on and off on its own. Beer glasses have been known to move themselves (waitstaff typically have to hold them in place under the tap so they won't move), and the doors have been known to open and close on their own. The most jaw-dropping story is from a non-believer. This skeptic was loudly proclaiming his disbelief of ghosts in the bar area when a piece of the tavern (the cover of the a/c unit) flew ten feet across the room and grazed him on the head. Besides the tavern, a variety of paranormal activity has been reported in other places throughout the inn.

People have reported feeling an unseen someone sit down on the bed next to them. They've also described seeing things out of the corner of their eyes. Multiple reports have been made of unusual cold spots and cold drafts felt in different locations throughout the Inn, coming from no obvious source. Lights turn on and off in the dining room and elsewhere. Employees recently have been hearing their names whispered from some disembodied source.

Final Impressions

The beautiful old Yarmouth and is a must-see while visiting Cape Cod. You'll be treated to amazing hospitality, and seafood consistently rated excellent on most travel sites. Plus, you never know, you may get a surprise spectral foot rub or come face-to-face with one of their resident haunts.

MASSACHUSSETS

SPIRITS OF THE SPOONER HOUSE
The Spooner House, Plymouth, Massachusetts

Plymouth Massachusetts has been called "America's hometown". It's of course known for the Mayflower and the Pilgrims landing site. It's also known for a variety of beautiful coastal homes in the area. One of these homes, The Spooner House, is a two story beauty over 200 years old and one street over from where the Pilgrims built their settlement. The Spooner House is a popular historic site, museum, and apparently, a Historic Haunt.

Spooner House postcard collection of the author

Originally built in 1749 for widow Hannah Jackson; it came into the possession of the Spooner family. Five Spooner generations called the house home. The first Spooner to reside here was American Revolutionary War patriot Deacon Ephraim Spooner. The home remained in the family until 1954. In that year, James Spooner, a lifelong bachelor and music patron passed, the last member of the family to occupy the house. James bequeathed his home, furnishings, and generations of family possessions to be incorporated into a historical museum. While many generations of Spooners occupied the home, and despite some rumors, there were few historically noted incidents or accidents that might definitely help explain some of the unusual activity there, save one big one.

A Blight on the Family Name

Long before James Spooner left the house to be converted into a museum, and after Deacon Ephraim Spooner helped accentuate the importance of protecting "Plymouth Rock", and the colonies, another incident forever marked the Spooner name. Joshua Spooner, a wealthy farmer, had taken a bride in an arranged marriage, her name was Bathsheba Ruggles. The two had four children together by the time the Revolution was underway in 1776. Bathsheba developed an utter aversion to the man she married who she knew to be abusive. In the spring of 1777, Ezra Ross, a 16 year old soldier in the Continental Army, fell ill in route to his farm in Massachusetts. Bathsheba nursed him back to health. He became friends of the family visiting on travels to and from Army service and traveling with Joshua Spooner on business trips. During this time he also had an affair with Bathsheba. She became pregnant.

43

MASSACHUSSETS
Historic Haunts of the North II

Bathsheba, knowing the punishment for adultery was at the very least, to have your clothes removed from the waist up and be whipped, urged Ross to kill her abusive husband. On a trip in February of 1778, Ross accompanied Joshua Spooner on a long trip to Princeton, Massachusetts. Bathsheba had given Ross a bottle of nitric acid and asked him to use it to poison Spooner. Ross, could not in good conscience do it. He backed out of her plan and returned immediately to his home in Linebrook.

Perhaps sensing that Ross would be unable to carry out her plan, Bathsheba invited two runaway British soldiers, Pvt. Williams Brooks and Sgt. James Buchanan, to sup and stay at the Spooner home. There she discussed ideas for killing her husband with the men. Having successfully convinced the men to aid her, she wrote Ross to inform him of the new plot. It has been implied that the attractive Bathsheba may have flirted and made impure suggestions to the men to help coerce them into going along with her plans.

Not long after, Joshua Spooner returned home, blissfully unaware of the original plot to kill him, and the newest one hatched by his wife and her coconspirators. The following evening after his return, Spooner came home after a night of drinking and debauchery at a local tavern. When he returned home, Brooks and Buchanan brutally beat him to death. The two men hid the body (with the help of Ross) in Spooners' Well. After the murder, Bathsheba had the men open her husband's lockbox and distributed money and articles of his clothing to them. On a whim, the men took one of Joshua Spooners' horses and traveled about 14 miles away to nearby Worcester. The next day Spooner's body was found. The two murderers drew attention to themselves by drinking, bragging, and flashing buckles and other items with Joshua Spooner's initials on them. The men were soon discovered and rounded up.

The four were put on trial. Robert Treat Paine, a signer of the Declaration of Independence, conducted the prosecution. The trial was marked by several noteworthy and historical events new to the American judicial system. At the onset, it was the original in American jurisprudence in which a plea of insanity was made. Bathsheba's lawyer claimed she had a "disordered mind," and was clearly mad! This clearly caused her to act irrationally. He claimed for proof you needed to look no further than the fact that the plan was poorly conceived with no well made plans for the perpetrators to escape capture.

For his part, Ross claimed that he shouldn't be held to the same standards as the other men since he didn't commit the crime. Despite Ross' protests, the three men were found guilty of murdering Joshua Spooner. Spooner's wife, Bathsheba, was found guilty of being an accessory to the crime. The four were sentenced to death and the execution was set for June 4, 1778.

Bathsheba attempted to put off the execution by informing the court she was pregnant. Two male midwives and a panel of 12 women examined her. They all swore that she was not "quick with child." Bathsheba and her con-

MASSACHUSSETS
Spirits of the Spooner House

fessor (the Rev. Thaddeus Maccarty), protested the report. Four examiners and another midwife, along with Bathsheba's brother-in-law, Dr. John Green, conducted a second examination and supported the claim of pregnancy. As a result, she sought a stay of execution to deliver her baby, the Massachusetts Council rejected her petition. They did not believe she was pregnant. Bathsheba, along with Ross, Brooks, and Buchanan, were hanged on July 2 in Worcester's Washington Square before a crowd of 5000 spectators. She was thirty-three years old. Newspapers described the case as "the most extraordinary crime ever perpetrated in New England." The former Mrs. Spooner was the first woman executed in the newly minted America! A post-mortem examination, performed as Bathsheba's last request, showed that she was pregnant with "a perfect male fetus of the growth of five months."

There has been some questioning of the motivation and validity of the opinions of the panel who originally examined Bathsheba for pregnancy, as well as the motivation of the Massachusetts Executive Council. Bathsheba, like her father, was a known Loyalist to England (unlike her dead husband). It has been suggested that she was executed, at least partially, based on the community's hostility towards the English leanings she and her father shared.

The Haunted Spooner House

The Spooner family experienced other unfortunate incidents besides Bathsheba, the details of which are only known in a few situations. However, at least two family members are thought to still be spiritually residing there. In 2005, workmen came to the house to do repairs and knocked on the door. A little girl in colonial clothing answered the door and allowed them in. The crew went to work. Shortly thereafter, the curator came in and asked the men how they had gotten into the house without him. They answered that the little girl had let them in. The curator informed them there was no little girl, not a living one anyway. The workmen packed up and left.

The little girl's spirit is often seen at the house. The little girl is allegedly known as Abigail Townsend. According to some reports the Spooner's took her in some time in the mid-1800s to raise her. Unfortunately, when she was about eight years old she died from a severe tooth infection in one of the upstairs bedrooms. Abigail is said to be very playful (and apparently helpful since she allowed the workmen in). She has also been seen looking down from the second floor window. Many guests have reported seeing a young child peering from the window, then vanishing before their eyes. Her apparition has also been seen standing at the corner of the house. Several tour groups have encountered her spirit before watching her dissapear before them. Fairly recently she had been reported "visiting" at least one neighbor. A neighbor who by all accounts, often encountered this intelligent haunt and has since moved!

MASSACHUSSETS
Historic Haunts of the North II

Besides Abigail, James Spooner's spirit is also said to still be here. He was a lover of music and often times when the museum is closed people have reported hearing the sound of music coming from inside. There have been several reports detailing incidents that happen when employees of the Museum are closing down at night. They describe hearing voices or music coming from another room. They investigate, but find no living soul there other than themselves. They are completely alone in the house or are they?

There have also been paranormal reports of lights coming from inside the house described like candles or lanterns going from room to room at night when the place is closed and empty. Interestingly enough, one tour group tried to shine a light through the shutters to get a look inside and were startled by the shutters being suddenly flung open by a woman who was staring at them before she vanished into thin air. Not surprising, this caused the onlookers to flee. Some have speculated that the "woman's ghost" could be Bathsheba.

The Unusual Grave Markers

There are two grave markers related to this unusual tale. While they may or may not be haunted, both have exhibited some interesting qualities. The first is the marker for Spooner Well, where the conspirators threw Joshua Spooner's dead body. This now infamous well, which is still visible off East Main Street in Brookfield, is typically covered with poison ivy that, despite applications of herbicides and other eradication methods, continues to grow.

The second marker indicates the final resting place for Joshua Spooner once his body was removed from the well. The area where the grave marker is positioned is considered fairly fertile soil. However, Joshua Spooner was considered such a nasty man that, according to legend, grass never grows on his grave site.

Final Thoughts

Ghost stories aside, the Spooner House is a very interesting piece of Plymouth Massachusetts history. One I encourage all history buffs to explore. I haven't been able to do a full blown investigation at the house and grounds of this Historic Haunt myself, but hope to one day. If I do, perhaps I'll bring a small toy or trinket, a musical one, in the hopes that Abigail's ghost wants to play or that James may come out and jam.

MASSACHUSSETS

SPIRITS OF STONE'S PUBLIC HOUSE
Stone's Public House, Ashland, Massachusetts

Massachusetts has no shortage of reportedly haunted locations. However, one that repeatedly comes up and has been visited by numerous psychics, seers, mystics, and ghost hunting groups is Stone's Public House in Ashland. The details of these haunts are as interesting as the iconic pub itself.

*Stone's Public House
courtesy of Wikipedia Creative Commons*

History of Stone's Public House

John Stone was already a successful farmer, former captain in the militia, and savvy businessman when he heard the railroad was going to build through the center of town and his property. Stone had owned most of the land in the center of town. It was then called Unionville (it is now called Ashland).

By Stone's reckoning a new hotel was greatly needed, so he would build it near the tracks. He began construction in 1832 and completed it in 1834. It reportedly opened to much fan fare with 300 guests attending, plenty of them eager to stay at the new Railroad Boarding House, or simply Railroad House.

John Stone operated the Railroad House for less than two years, but leased it to many innkeepers until his death in 1858. Stone also built a residence nearby, but frequented the Railroad House often. W. A. Scott bought the inn in 1868. However, he could not maintain it and after his ownership it went through many hands.

In 1976 Leonard "Cappy" Fournier bought and restored the building, Fournier and his people began to experience several unusual things happening at the former Railroad House (now renamed Stone's Public House in honor of the original founder). These could have been stirred up by the renovations, but the activity was definitely paranormal in nature and led Fournier to investigate for himself.

MASSACHUSSETS
Historic Haunts of the North II

Fournier's Research and Details of the Other Haunts

Fournier was the first to research the Stone's paranormal reports. Upon researching he discovered that in the 1890s a drunkard by the name of Burt Philips possibly died at the inn. Many believe he is one of the resident ghosts here. Psychics claim he refuses to leave because he likes the atmosphere of the bar, and that he's responsible for reports of disembodied cold hands some patrons at the bar have experienced on their necks. Apparently Philips still likes to belly up to the bar.

Many of the Public House's employees do not like, or even refuse to be by themselves alone at night. Bartenders have reported seeing water taps at the bar turn off and on by themselves. They've also described doors that swing themselves open or shut. These doors, when bolted to prevent the unusual activity, refuse to stay bolted. Glasses have been reported to fly off the shelves or mysteriously crack and shatter in place with no obvious explanations. Could this be Burt Philips up to his drunken antics? Possibly, but there are reports of seven or more spirits at the inn.

Many patrons and staff claim that one of the resident ghosts may be John Stone himself. There are numerous reports of paranormal activity centered near Stone's image in the bar. These reports vary from vague uneasiness in its vicinity to phantom cigar smoke. Many feel that Stone's spirit is here bound by what began in an upstairs room at the house.

The Story of Mike McPherson

Mike McPherson was a salesman from New York staying at the boarding house, who asked to play in a friendly card game going on between Stone and some of his friends and employees. McPherson became the big winner of the night cleaning everyone out of reportedly several thousand dollars in winnings. A plot was hatched by the losers at the table (who were convinced he was cheating) to club him on the head, remove his valuables and dump him outside the Boarding House to recover after learning his lesson. However, all did not go as planned. The blow to the head meant to knock him out, killed him instead. Six or seven others were supposedly involved and helped hide the body. Many details of the story have since been corroborated. Most of the other ghosts said to inhabit the Public House are the conspirators whose spirits are apparently trapped here by their actions. Among these ghosts is the spirit of the chambermaid, Sadie, who revealed the story by spilling some of the details to visiting psychics.

The Sad Tale of Mary Smith

Another ghost said to inhabit Stone's Public House is that of a little Irish girl named Mary Smith. Her spirit has been encountered giggling, casting shadows, peering through windows, and disappearing into the walls. The story behind this little girl's haunting is much more tragic than the details behind her innocent haunting.

Mary was apparently playing too close to the tracks and was killed by a train car (the official cause of death was listed as car, there were no automobiles at the time, the only "cars" were train cars). Someone at the Boarding House must have spotted the accident. Mary was brought inside and a doctor was sent for, but it was too late.

Mary's blood stained linen pinafore is reportedly kept at Stone's in the attic. One female employee reportedly took the dress home. However, she found herself immediately immersed in so much paranormal activity at her place that she brought the dress back.

It's stories like these of Mary Smith and Mike McPherson, that draw the curious general public, and those in the paranormal field alike to Stone's. A very popular paranormal television show even filmed an episode here. The Stone's staff called the team in to investigate some of the reports and occurrences they experienced for themselves. The team had some fantastic ghostly encounters of their own. There were reports of the crew being touched by unseen hands, and hearing disembodied voices during the investigation. There were even reports of a little girl's apparition seen by the railroad tracks (the same perhaps who died there in an accident). The film crew even caught some ghostly phenomenon on film. They reportedly captured images of the little girl's shadow.

If you're in the area of Ashland Massachusetts and you're looking to capture a good memory, this is the place. Stone's food and fun atmosphere is notorious. If you're a fan of the paranormal, Stone's Public House is a must stop on your historic or haunted tour of Massachusetts.

NEW HAMPSHIRE

THE PHANTOM PRINCESS OF MOUNT WASHINGTON

Mount Washington Resort, Bretton Woods, NH

In Northern New Hampshire, in the town of Bretton Woods, there lies a historic luxury resort hotel. This hotel, Mount Washington, is well known for playing a crucial part in the creation of the International Monetary Fund. It's well known to past guests for it's amenities and universally enjoyable experience. New guests will no doubt discover for themselves; however, they may also discover firsthand, that the resort is haunted.

Mount Washington Resort courtesy of rickpilot Wikipedia Creative Commons

Mount Washington's History and Where it Got its Name

One of the more prominent peaks in the White Mountains of New Hampshire is the highest mountaintop in the Northeastern United States. It was named by early scholars/climbers of the time, Mount Washington, in honor of President George Washington. Over time, seven of the thirteen mountains in the range would be named for past Presidents. In fact, the range itself would be come to be called The Presidential Ridge, hoping to inspire local residents and history lovers. Just as George Washington inspired the naming of the the largest of these majestic mountains, this mountain and its proximity, would inspire the building of a grand hotel. The Mount Washington Hotel was constructed between 1900 and 1902.

The hotel was built by Joseph Stickney, a Pennsylvania railroad tycoon who has also made his fortune from investments, including in coal mining. As a result, Stickney and his partner John N. Conyngham, spared no expense in its construction. Stickney brought in 250 Italian artisans to work on the place. He also had a private room and dining room built for his wonderful wife Carolyn. The Stickneys very quickly fell in love with their new hotel. Unfortunately, not long after its completion, Joseph Stickney died in December of 1903, from a sudden heart attack. After Stickney's death, Carolyn Foster Stickney inherited the hotel.

NEW HAMPSHIRE
The Phantom Princess of Mount Washington

*Princess Carolyn
Public Domain*

Carolyn's Time in Charge

Carolyn seemed to focus her energies after her husband's passing on her beloved hotel. She added the Sun Dining Room, and additional guest rooms. She also added a fourth floor between the towers, and built the Stickney Memorial Chapel in honor of her late husband.

Several years after Joseph Stickney's passing Carolyn met and became romantically linked to French Royal Jean Baptiste Marie de Faucigny Lucinge. The two married in 1908. Among the elites, aristocracy, and others he was known as Prince Lucinge of France, and thus she began to be called Princess Carolyn. After the wedding ceremony, Princess Carolyn moved to Europe to be with her new groom. The French would discover (as her friends here already knew), that Carolyn was a generous and kind soul. For her philanthropic efforts in France during the terrible war, she was decorated with the **Crox de Guerre** with palms, a very prestigious award given to those who have distinguished themselves with acts of heroism.

The Prince would serve with the French Army as Captain of the Cavalry in World War I. He would be awarded the Army **Distinguished Service Medal**. Unfortunately, only a handful of years after the end of the war, the Prince would pass in 1922.

Princess Carolyn moved back to the resort she loved after Prince Lucinge's death. She would spend the rest of her days at her treasured hotel. She also made arrangements in Old North Cemetery in Concord, New Hampshire, to allow a mausoleum to be built. In this place she would eventually be interred with another fan of the hotel, her first husband, Joseph Stickney.

For a time the Mount Washington hotel thrived. The advent of income tax, Prohibition, and the Great Depression would see the hotel's fortunes change for the worse. In 1936, Princess Carolyn passed. Her nephew, Foster Reynolds would inherit the hotel that same year.

The hotel would close in 1942 with the coming of World War II. Later, in 1944, a Boston Syndicate purchased the extensive property. That same year the hotel hosted the **Bretton Wood International Monetary Conference**. During the conference, representatives from 44 nations met to establish the **World Bank** and **International Monetary Fund**, setting the U.S. Dollar as the main currency. Documents for those landmark organizations were signed in the hotel's Gold Room. For each

*The Gold Room
courtesy of Barry Livingstone
Wikipedia Creative Commons*

51

NEW HAMPSHIRE
Historic Haunts of the North II

bedroom that housed a conference guest, a plaque was placed outside the door detailing which country's representative stayed there.

Mount Washington Resort continued to serve her guests with distinction. In 1975, the hotel was added to the National Register of Historic Places. In 1986, it was recognized as a National Historic Landmark. In 1991, the property was purchased by a group of New Hampshire businessmen. In 1999, the building was overhauled, others on property were renovated, and new ones added. By 2006, Bretton Wood's mountain retreat included some 991 acres.

Today, the property includes several hotels and lodges, and ski and golf areas. It contains about 200 guest rooms and suites in total. It boasts meeting spaces, a full service spa and salon, and a slew of other amenities. It seemingly has its own famous ghost and a remarkable amout of paranormal activity.

*Mount Washington Resort Presidential wing
courtesy of Barry Livingstone Wikipedia Creative Commons*

Paranormal Activity at Mount Washington

Many hotel guests and staff have described unusual phenomenon at the hotel. The tower suite lights are known to turn off and on. The smell of fragrant perfume springs up suddenly and drifts into rooms with no obvious source for the scent. Objects have also been known to disappear, only to reappear later in the same place. Even some of the bathtubs seem to have a metaphysical mind of their own. They've been known to have their taps mysteriously turn on (as if by invisible hands) to fill up wth water. More startling than tubs and their taps, is the frequently seen apparition of an elegant woman spotted in Victorian dress. The staff are sure it's Princess Carolyn.

52

NEW HAMPSHIRE
The Phantom Princess of Mount Washington

Princess Carolyn's Ghost

Staff and guests of the Mount Washington have frequently claimed to see an apparition looking over the balcony of the hotel that matches Princess Carolyn's description. An idea that seems to be supported buy the spirit's actions in these instances, as Carolyn used to stand on these balconies and look at what the guests were wearing so that she could dress herself up to outshine them. She has also been spotted, transparent, descending the stairs for dinner. However, she's more frequently encountered by guests and staff in her old suite, Room #314.

The Princess Room

Room #314 is called the "Princess Room" and was Carolyn's private suite when she was alive. In that room is a four poster bed, the same one she shared with her first husband. It's said that she loved it so much, that she reportedly had it shipped wherever she traveled.

Guests have detailed numerous encounters with the Princess. In most, the startled guests awaken in the middle of the night to see her apparition at the end of the bed, slowly brushing her hair. They've also mentioned the fact that she likes to give a disembodied "nudge" once in a while (perhaps trying to make room for herself in the bed). She has even been captured in photos looking out one of the windows in the Princess' Room.

A Few Last Things About the Mount Washington Resort

The hotel has such a reputation for its haunted nature, that it has been featured on several paranormal television shows. These ghost hunters have even claimed to capture EVP's of a successful question and answer session with Princess Carolyn. Whether you visit the resort as a ghost hunter or guest, you're sure to be impressed with this expansive property, its amenities, and two Four Diamond Rated dining rooms. It's not just a member in good standing of the Historic Hotels of America, it's a member in good standing of my Historic Haunts.

NEW JERSEY

THE HAUNTING TALE AND TRAGIC LOSSES OF THE HINDENBURG
Manchester Township, New Jersey

Most of us have seen blimps on television or floating over sporting events. At one time these gas filled giants were poised to become the next big thing in air travel. That all changed on a rainy May night in 1937, in New Jersey, when scenes of a horrific accident were captured on film. The incident would haunt the public perception, and the field where the incident occurred. Hindenburg, the pride of German engineering, had gone from humble beginnings to a ball of flames! Let's take a closer look at how it got to that point and the otherworldly impression it's left on the area.

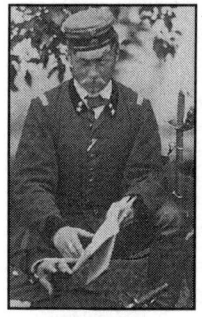

Hindenburg on fire Public domain

The Hindenburg's Origin

In 1863, a young German engineering student was acting as an observer in the Civil War for the Union's Army of the Potomac. His name was Ferdinand von Zeppelin. In the course of his travels he met German-born balloonist John Skiner and made an aerial ascent with him in a balloon. This would energize Zeppelin's interest in aeronautics. He would found a company that would pioneer rigid airships. Several countries would dabble in airships, especially as bombers during the first World War. After the war by 1930, most had given up, citing accidents and other shortcomings. However, Germany, and Zeppelin in particular, had not given up the ghost and were still in pursuit of a superior airship.

By the late 1920s Zeppelin had succeeded in creating a large impressive airship with material stretched over a rigid frame called **Graf Zeppelin** (LZ 127). This airship offered the first commercial transatlantic passenger flight service. Its success led to the creation of the longest class ship of the line and largest airship by volume **Hindenburg**. The Hindenburg was named after Field Marshal

Zeppelin during Civil War Public Domain

Ferdinand von Zeppelin Nicola Perscheid Creative Commons

54

NEW JERSEY
The Haunting Tale of the Hindenburg

Paul Von Hindenburg, president of Germany from 1925 until his death in 1934. LZ129 Hindenburg (Luftshiff Zeppelin #129) was a German, commercial passenger-carrying, rigid airship, at the time they were known as dirigibles.

The Hindenburg Takes Flight

The Hindenburg first flew in March of 1936. The airship was over 800 feet long, and weighed approximately 250 tons. She was carried aloft by 16 gas cells with combustible hydrogen (a lighter-than-air gas) for lift. Hindenburg, the fastest airship of its kind, normally operated at speeds of 84 mph, but with favorable winds could accelerate up to 188 mph.

Tickets for passage on the aircraft were extremely expensive. Hindenburg catered to its travelers with 25 cabins and amenities including: a dining room where grand meals were served, a lounge, writing room, a smoker's lounge, and bar. These passengers also enjoyed panoramic windows with spectacular views of the countryside as the ship flew over. The Hindenburg was considered the pinnacle of "Superior German Engineering". Gaining worldwide fame, she served as a propaganda tool for the German government, and a luxurious means of making a transatlantic journey.

The Hindenburg made several transatlantic trips from Frankfurt to various locations in 1936. In fact, she had made ten uneventful trips to the U.S. where she arrived and moored in NAS Lakehurst, Manchester Township, New Jersey. The airship had begun its 1937 season with a successful round trip passage to Rio de Janeiro, Brazil.

The Zeppelin company promoted their voyages by publicizing, among other things, the fact that no passenger had been injured on any of their airships. Like the Titanic, and almost as large, she received an extraordinary amount of publicity as she departed Frankfurt, Germany on the evening of May 3rd. This would be the first of ten scheduled round trips between Europe and the U.S. American Airlines had contracted with the Hindenburg to shuttle passengers from Lakehurst to Newark for connecting airplane flights.

Bundes Archives
Hindenburg Dining Area
with large windows
Creative Commons

Hindenburg over Lakehurst
with Hanger 1 in 1936
Public Domain Image

Hindenburg's Gondola
at Lakehurst after 1936 flight
Creative Commons

55

NEW JERSEY
Historic Haunts of the North II

*Hindenburg with reporters around it
Public Domain*

The Collected Press

Everywhere she went the Hindenburg made news and the German government made sure she stayed in the public eye. As her 1937 travel season had begun, and as she made her way to America, there was a large group of press that had gathered to cover the event. After all, she was the flight of the year. Cameramen from four newsreel teams were gathered along with photographers, journalists, spectators, and others to film the landing.

Among the press corps present for coverage were radio broadcaster Herbert Morrison and engineer Charlie Nehlsen. Station WLS in Chicago had sent them there to cover the airship's May 6th arrival.

The Early Days of the Hindenburg Journey

The Hindenburg experienced storms and strong headwinds on its way to America that put it behind schedule (a concern since it was fully booked for its return flight). In fact, the Zeppelin was well behind schedule when it passed over Boston the morning of May 6th. Afternoon thunderstorms and poor weather conditions at the Lakehurst landing site delayed the arrival even more. Captain Max Pruss decided to bide his time to give atmospheric conditions a chance to clear up. He charted a course over Manhattan Island (which caused quite the public spectacle). Afterward, he passed over the landing site at 4 pm, but the weather was still too bad to attempt to bring the airship in.

Captain Pruss again had to stall and wait for the weather to clear. He took passengers over the New Jersey seashore. The Captain was notified at 6:22 pm that the storms had passed and they could head back to Lakehurst. At this time they were almost a half a day late. This left less time to service and prepare the ship for its scheduled flight back to Europe. The public was informed that because of this, they would not be permitted at the mooring location or to board the ship, while it briefly stayed in port in nearby Hanger 1. This thankfully, may have saved more lives. The Hindenburg began its final approach to Lakehurst at 7 pm.

The Beginning of the End

The decision was made to do a "flying moor" or high landing in which the Zeppelin would drop its landing ropes and mooring cables from a higher altitude and then be winched down to the awaiting mooring mast. This would take more time initially, but could allow for less ground crew (which again may have saved lives). The Hindenburg had only performed this maneuver at Lakehurst a few times in 1936. Sudden and shifting winds forced the aircraft to make several sharp turns in an effort to get back on its flightpath for mooring; something it wasn't great at and that could have damaged the ship. Now back on course, the mooring lines were dropped at 7:21 pm as a light rain began to fall.

NEW JERSEY
The Haunting Tale of the Hindenburg

At 7:25 pm witnesses saw fabric of the upper fin fluttering as if gas was leaking from the aircraft. At about this same moment others claimed to see dim blue flames or St. Elmo's Fire on the top and back of the ship. Passengers on board heard muffled detonations, and those in the front of the ship felt a sudden shock. Gas cells onboard the aircraft began to catch fire. The structure's rear end imploded. The Hindenburg was quickly becoming engulfed in flames! She began to fall from the sky.

The Hindenburg's bow lurched upward. The Zeppelin's back broke and the tail end came crashing to the ground. Flame burst through the nose of the ship (killing 9 of 12 crewmen there). Fire continued to swallow the aircraft. The fabric on the hull burned away and the bow and gondola came crashing to the ground. Most of the officers lept through the windows as the bow crashed. The Hindenburg then rolled slightly to the side cutting off escape of starboard passengers. Tragically, the total time from the first signs of trouble to the bow crashing to the ground was between 32 and 37 seconds! The Hindenburg was engulfed in flames. The proud ship that had once flown millionaires like Nelson Rockefeller, and soared over the Olympic Stadium in Berlin, was no more.

Incredible Escapes, Heroic Rescues, and a High Body Count

Several people died trying to jump from the doomed ship at excessive altitudes. A vaudeville acrobat named Joseph Späh hung onto one of the aircraft's window ledges and let go when it was 20 feet from the ground. He executed an acrobat's safety roll and injured his ankle, after getting help, he survived.

Chief Petty Officer Frederick J. "Bull" Tobin— a survivor from another airship crash, the USS Shenandoah—was in command of the airship's navy landing party. Without hesitation he shouted the order "Navy men, Stand fast!" He rallied the frightened personnel to rush in and conduct rescue operations despite the flames. Gangway stairs were used by these men to rescue a number of passengers.

As the rescuers sprang into action, the Hindenburg's First Officer found Captain Pruss, very badly burned and attempting to re-enter the wreckage to look for survivors. Pruss would later require hospitalization and

*Hindenburg Tragedy
All Public Domain*

NEW JERSEY
Historic Haunts of the North II

reconstructive surgery. Many other crewmen would also endure bad burns and survive the initial accident only to die later in the hospital. Of the 97 total individuals onboard at that fateful moment, there were 35 fatalities (13 passengers and 22 crewman). Another individual, a member of the ground crew, was killed as well. The terrible and public deaths of so many would soon be front page news.

"Oh the Humanity"
Unfortunately, the collected press, prepared for the landing, had a front row seat for the accident. Photographers captured heartbreaking pictures. Newsreel companies filmed the incident in all it's brutal detail. Herbert Morrison and his engineer Charlie Nehlsen would record the event (a process then in its infancy) in what is considered one of the most heartbreaking and important broadcasts in history. As transcribed here...

"It's starting to rain again; it's... the rain had (oh) slacked up a little bit. The back motors of the ship are just holding it (uh) just enough to keep it from...It's burst into flames! Get this, Charlie; get this, Charlie! It's fire, and it's crashing! It's crashing, terrible! Oh, my! Get out of the way, please! It's burning, bursting into flames and the... and it's falling on the mooring mast and all the folks between it. This is terrible, this is one of the worst catastrophes in the world. Oh it's... [unintelligible] its flames... Crashing, oh! Four- or five-hundred feet into the sky and it... it's a terrific crash, ladies and gentlemen. It's smoke, and it's flames now; and the frame is crashing to the ground, not quite to the mooring mast. Oh, the humanity, all the passengers. screaming around here. I told you: it... I can't even talk to people, their friends are on there! Ah! It's... it... it's a... ah! I... I can't talk, ladies and gentlemen. Honest: it's just laying there, mass of smoking wreckage. Ah! And everybody can hardly breathe and talk and the screaming, lady, I... I... I'm sorry. Honest, I... I can hardly breathe. I... I'm going to step inside, where I cannot see it. Charlie, that's terrible. Ah, ah... I can't, I... Listen, folks: I... I'm gonna have to stop for a minute because I've lost my voice. This is the worst thing I've ever witnessed."
—Herbert Morrison, [radio broadcast transcribed] May 6th, Lakehurst, New Jersey

After several pauses to collect himself, Morrison and the engineer reported on the rescue efforts, interviewed survivors, and shared details of the tragedy. Their recordings were rushed back to Chicago by airplane later that night, and broadcast in full. The next day, NBC Radio would rebroadcast portions nationally. This marked the first time recordings of a news event were ever broadcast, and the first coast-to-coast radio broadcast as well. The newsreel footage would be paired with Morrison's passionate reporting and seen throughout America and the world. This effectively shattered industry faith and the public's perception of airships. The footage, combined together with the success of fledgling international air travel company Pan-Am (see **Historic Haunts of the South III** for more), marked the end of the commercial passenger zeppelins.

NEW JERSEY
The Haunting Tale of the Hindenburg

The Immediate Aftermath of the Hindenburg Crash

While the hydrogen burned up quickly, it took several hours for the Hindenburg's diesel fuel to burn out. Hanger 1 at Lakehurst Naval Base, the building that had housed the Zeppelin on prior flights, now housed many of the wounded and the dead (with the crew's quarters in the hanger becoming something of a morgue). From here many were taken to the nearby military hospital. As for the Hindenburg, smoke was still rising from the ship's twisted and scorched metal skeleton the next day.

The Inquiries Begin, Theories are Tested

Wild speculation began for causes of the accident. The New York Daily News even listed five theories for the demise of the dirigible including lightning, backfiring engine, ground crew issues, a spark, or an act of God! Days after the incident, to get to the bottom of it, a board of inquiry was set up at Lakehurst. The U.S. was represented by Colonel South Trimble Jr. The German Commission was headed by Hugo Eckener.

Hindenburg Tragedy
Wikimedia Creative Commons

Eckener worked with the Zeppelin group and mentioned the group receiving threatening letters before the accident. As a result, he and several others (including Captain Pruss) felt the Hindenburg might have been destroyed as an act of sabotage. Proponents of this theory put forth the acrobat who escaped, Joseph Späh, as a suspect, and Erich Spehl, a rigger on the Hindenburg who later died from his burns in the infirmary. No credible evidence of sabotage could be found.

The other theory that gained traction was that the accident was caused by a build up of static electricity on the zeppelin that may have ignited the ship. Hindenburg had passed through several weather fronts and could easily have been carrying a high electrical charge. The German scientists after testing, concluded the wet insulation of the outer covering of the airship most likely caused a spark which jumped to a metal piece and ignited the hydrogen. This would suggest there was a design flaw in Germany's "superior aircraft", the report was burned. The inquiry ended with the finding that the rather vague culprit was "atmospheric conditions"

After the Accident and Theories Since

Part of Hindenburg's framework was salvaged

Hindenburg Wreckage
Public Domain

59

NEW JERSEY
Historic Haunts of the North II

and returned to Germany. It was recycled into military aircraft. Many of these aircraft also reportedly experienced "incidents" and unusually bad luck.

Since the time of the tragic accident, other theories have been investigated and tested. Including "incendiary paint" believed to be present on the outer fabric of the Hindenburg. Scientists and other specialists at NASA and elsewhere, meticulously attempted to recreate the incident on numerous occasions since that terrible day. From these experiments there have been more suggestions for the cause including, a puncture in the hull, a fuel leak, or a weapon fired at the ship. The case remains a mystery although many believe it may have been a mixture of several elements.

Hindenburg Memorial Marker
Hanger 1 in background
Public Domain

Hindenburg Memorial Marker
photographer paxswill
Wikimedia Creative Commons

Hindenburg, Memorials and Passed Passengers

The site was designated a National Historic Landmark in 1968. On May 6, 1987 (the 50th Anniversary) memorial markers, including a brass plaque where the gondola landed, and markers at Hanger 1 were dedicated.

We will probably never know what happened for sure as the last crew member Werner Franz (a 14 year old cabin boy at the time) passed away in 2014. In December 2019, the last passenger, Werner Doehner (a child at the time, thrown to safety by his mother) died. To this day the Hindenburg still haunts our collective conscience, and apparently the area where the aircraft went down.

Hindenburg's Haunts

Even before Hindenburg, Lakehurst Naval Base was already thought to be haunted. There have been reports of strange lights, unusual objects, and even ghostly encounters. However, numerous witness accounts would suggest that the crash site, Hanger 1, and the hospital that ultimately treated the victims, are all very paranormally active.

The hospital that treated the injured from Hindenburg (some of them died later of their wounds) has been thought to be haunted for some time. Strange things happen here frequently that are hard to explain. The hospital often experiences mysterious footsteps, disembodied voices, rattling doors, loud crashing noises,

NEW JERSEY
The Haunting Tale of the Hindenburg

and lights that turn themselves off and on. Some believe the sad souls of the Hindenburg are haunting it, many of whom were brought here from Hanger 1.

The Haunts of Hanger 1 and the Crash Site

Hanger 1 has been known to be very paranormally active. Shadow figures have been seen, footsteps heard, and even the sounds of crying encountered. Several men stationed there and others visiting the area swear the hanger is haunted. They describe unusual things that happen there and a bad vibe that seems to emanate from the impromptu site of Hindenburg's morgue. The sounds of disembodied footsteps are common (especially in the rafters). The activity has, at times, been so intense, it's chased groups of burly military men from the building. With all this activity, Hanger 1 still pales when compared to the Hindenburg crash site.

The Hindenburg crash site has been featured on several television shows. Many have claimed to capture evidence with their equipment. The area is known to be extremely paranormally active.

The crash site has had many active reports of heavy screams and cries. Witnesses have reportedly "smelled" the fire, felt the heat, or encountered something very large, hovering over them. There have even been some who have reported seeing the Hindenburg ablaze on the anniversary of the event. Many in the paranormal believe the souls of Hindenburg's dead may still linger.

Personal Connections and My Final Thoughts

I know a couple of people who grew up near the site and have visited the area. They don't know each other, and they lived here at completly different times. However, both have claimed the area has a heavy and intense sort of atmosphere, sad, and at times terrifying. Each of them in turn has claimed they heard the disturbing sounds of disembodied screams. Both also said at points they felt as if they were standing in front of a fire when they walked the area of the crash. They echo a common phenomenon among witnesses to the site.

Many involved in investigating the paranormal feel that traumatic accidents can leave residual energy, an imprint, resulying in ghostly activity or even a full blown haunting. The amount of emotional and psychic energy released by so many terrified people could easily have left an impression on the area or an intense residual haunting. Regardless of the paranormal occurrences, the Hindenburg incident is one of the most unfortunate in American history. Because of it, Lakehurst Naval Base has become a powerful Historic Haunt, and one not soon to be forgotten.

NEW YORK

THE AMITYVILLE HORROR HOUSE
House on Ocean Avenue, Amityville, New York

Who hasn't heard about the Amityville Horror? It is quite possibly the most recognized and famous case of a "haunted house" ever. The stories of the incidents that allegedly occurred to the Lutz family while living there, and the details of paranormal investigators later, remain perhaps the most intense, controversial, and divisive tales in the paranormal community.

To be honest —while deciding on locations for **Historic Haunts of the North**—I was on the fence about whether to include the house in Amityville or not. This is why it ended up in the second book. It has already received so much press, both positive and negative. One minute it's thought to be haunted, the next it isn't, (depending on who you talk to and what version of the story is in the public eye). It is arguably the most contentious story connected to the paranormal.

The Amityville House and high hopes during the time of the DeFeos

The reason I ultimately decided to include it is because I, like so many others, heard the story of the Amityville House, saw the movies, and read the book at a very early age. It was one of the many things that peaked my interest in the paranormal in my youth. Cases like this led me to investigate the supernatural and haunted locales. So I felt it deserved a spot in this book. This unusually long entry was arrived at by assembling details from numerous books, interviews, documentaries, movies, podcasts and the like, and my desire to give my readers enough information to form their own opinions.

The Lead Up to the Amityville Horror

Even before The Amityville Horror story, it had been suggested that this area was cursed, and that members of local Native American tribes thought the land could be a magnet for bad things and negative energy. Some believed there may have been a place here at one time for evil or mentally unstable members of the tribes. If so, they also believed these "undesirables" may have been buried here face down as was custom (a common theme in this story).

There was also speculation that the area might have been connected to John Ketchum, a practicing occultist and suspected witch reportedly driven from Salem around the time of the witch trials. He was rumored to have relocated to Amityville, and resumed his less than savory practices. While the exact area he may have operated in was unknown, the existence of a nearby street named for him (Ketchum Avenue) would seem to support this connection.

The house that sat at 112 Ocean Avenue was reportedly not the first. The first house was moved several blocks away because the owners of the home, the Moynahans, needed a bigger place for their family. Interestingly, the former House at Ocean Avenue (now relocated) —if past occupants are to be believed— experiences frequent paranormal activity itself, and may still be somehow connected to the area. That perhaps, is a story for another time.

The Moynahans obviously became more connected to the area when they had their large Dutch colonial home constructed in this suburban neighborhood of Amityville on the south shore of Long Island, New York. The Moynahans would live here until their deaths (both of natural causes). Their daughter would later sell the house. The family could have never suspected that the facade of their new home would become the iconic image it has.

The idea that the house or area might be cursed would come up again as subsequent owners of the house experienced unfortunate circumstances (especially near the boathouse). The Fitzgeralds moved in and ended up divorced with serious money problems. The Rileys would follow the Fitzgeralds in ownership and divorce. They would then sell the house to the DeFeo family.

The DeFeo Family Tragedy

Ronald DeFeo Sr. moved into the home with his wife and five children, including his eldest, Ronald "Ronnie" DeFeo, Jr. The elder DeFeo showered his kids with gifts and attention, and was excited to move here with his family. This was echoed in the sign he placed out front sporting the name "High Hopes". Despite these high hopes for a better life, rumors of problems in the house, abuse, and even possible mob connections began to emerge. It also became clear that there were problems between DeFeo Sr. and his son Ronnie.

Despite a stipend and minimal pressure for a full time job, over time Ronnie became bored, restless, and disconnected from his dad. He left several times. Each time he did, his dad would hunt him down and bring him back home. Ronnie began to argue with his father even more often. Feeling trapped Ronnie began to escape into drug use and alcohol. Much of this is known. However, subsequent examinations by authors, paranormal researchers, and investigative shows like ***In Search Of*** suggested that Ronnie began dabbling in witchcraft and possibly practiced animal sacrifice and devil worship.

For his part, Ronnie claimed to hear voices and weird sounds in the house. He claimed some kind of force in the house might have been trying to exert influence over him. Ronnie claimed, the unusual activity began shortly after Christmas of 1973.

Around this time the DeFeos reportedly began to notice paranormal activity in the home as well. The family allegedly sought religious help to cleanse the house

NEW YORK
Historic Haunts of the North II

of this activity. They reportedly found help in nearby Montréal. Ronald DeFeo Sr. informed the family he would have a priest come and do an exorcism. Ronnie refused to participate and left.

During the exorcism, candles reportedly moved and doors slammed shut. DeFeo allegedly told others he felt he had a "devil on his back". His wife, meanwhile, began to frequently tell friends and neighbors she thought something bad would happen to the family.

Not long after the attempted cleansing, Ronnie returned, and the tensions with his father again began to escalate. At one point, Ronnie reportedly held a loaded shotgun aimed at his father and pulled the trigger, but the gun miraculously failed to go off. DeFeo Sr. claimed it was "divine intervention". He traveled again to Montréal and began to accumulate religious statues and symbols of protection. He surrounded the house outside, and filled the house inside with them.

The Terrible Night

On November 13th, 1974 at around 3:15 a.m. Ronald DeFeo Jr. killed his parents and 4 siblings with a .35 caliber rifle. Ronnie shot his dad, then moved to the other side of the bed and shot his mother. He then left his parent's room and shot his brothers and sisters in their beds. There were several odd things about the murders. When the police toured the crime scene, all the victims were lying on their stomachs face down in bed. In addition, while some have suggested there may have been a thunderstorm that night, no one heard the shots in the house or next door, and none of the family woke up (it has been said that Ronnie may have drugged them with barbiturates). Ronnie then went to a local bar and asked for help claiming he had arrived home and found his family slaughtered.

At first, the police took Ronnie in for protection thinking it might be a mob killing since the crime scene had the look of mob style assassinations. Ronnie suggested this while being interviewed by the police, and even named potential culprits. However, there were no tell-tale signs of silencer use or drugs in the victim's systems that would explain why the family didn't wake with the loud gunshots, run, or fight back. By rights even the neighbors should have been alerted to the loud gunshots. It wasn't long before the police concluded there were way too many holes in the Ronnie DeFeo's story for it to be true.

Ronnie's story changed. He said that something awakened him that night and handed him the rifle. He also claimed that some force compelled him to do it and once he started, he couldn't stop.

DeFeo went on trial in October of 1975. His attorney claimed Ronnie had killed his family in self-defense because he heard their voices plotting to kill him. Ronnie's lawyer William Weber entered an insanity plea, but on November 21,

Ronnie DeFeo Mugshot Public Domain

1975, he was found guilty of six counts of 2nd degree murder and received six concurrent sentences of twenty-five years to life.

In prison, and during follow up interviews and retellings, Ronnie's story would change frequently. Ronnie even stated that his eldest sister Dawn had helped him with the murders before he shot her in self defense. There were unusual traces of gunpowder on her clothes, and some had suggested that fact alone merited more scrutiny of the case.

On other occasions Ronnie would again claim it was evil spirits in his head that told him to commit the murders. He admitted that while it wasn't that far-fetched to believe he might have killed his father (who he was known to have issues with), he would have never killed his mother or siblings unless under another influence. Many dismissed Ronnie's story and the "evil spirits" as side effects of the drugs he was taking at the time of the murders. Over the following years William Weber would continue to explore ways to help his client's case and to profit from it himself. Ronnie DeFeo would eventually die while still serving his sentence in March of 2021.

The Coming of the Lutz Family

In 1975, newlyweds George and Kathy Lutz and their family, were presented the former DeFeo residence after viewing several houses with real estate agents. The asking price was a ridiculously low $80,000 and they would soon learn why. The real estate agent was required to tell them, under the full disclosure rules, of the murders in the building. Despite this revelation, the whole family had reportedly already fallen in love with the place. They loved the immense size, the two car garage, the separate boathouse, and the swimming pool.

George & Kathy Lutz
Courtesy of GJ Fredbear/
Scarlet2435 & Amityville Wiki
Creative Commons (CC BY-SA)

The Lutzs held a family meeting to discuss purchasing the house. George claimed to be a non-practicing Methodist, and Kathy was a non-practicing Catholic at the time. They both considered themselves somewhat "spiritual" dabbling in Transcendentalism, meditation, and other "New Age" beliefs (especially George); but they considered themselves skeptics when it came to paranormal matters. They realized the only way they could afford a great house of that size was to deal with the house's history. If anything difficult did come up, George, a take charge guy, was an ex-marine with a black belt, and a reputation for pushing through tough situations. He felt he could handle it.

The family decided they wanted to buy the house. George and Kathy both owned their own homes at the time. However, they wanted a fresh start as a family. They sold their individual houses to make a bigger down payment and be "all in" on the new house. They rationalized they'd be saving money. They paid several months mortgage with the funds from the sale of their houses, and they were

NEW YORK
Historic Haunts of the North II

saving boat docking fees for George's boat (with the boathouse). George eventually planned to move his third-generation family surveying business into the basement, further saving office fees.

The Lutzs bought the home, and spent an additional $400 in the process which allowed them to buy much of the DeFeo family furnishings still there in the house, including some of the bed frames. The Lutzs reportedly asked to have all the DeFeo family religious items inside and out removed. A friend of George's who learned the history of the house recommended they have it blessed before fully moving in. George wasn't sure exactly what was involved, but he knew a priest who could do it and made arrangements for the priest to come. On December 18th of 1975, 29 year old George and Kathy moved in with Kathy's children from a previous marriage, Danny (age 10), Chris (age 7), and Melissa or "Missy" as they called her (age 5), and their crossbred Malamute/Labrador family dog named Harry.

Father Ray and the Talking House

As the Lutzs were moving in, they had a visit from Father Ralph Pecoraro nicknamed Father "Ray". Father Ray was an acquaintance of George Lutz. He was also the Ecclesiastical Judge for the Diocese of Rockville Centre, a lawyer, and a psychotherapist. Father Ray came with his Bible and holy water and began to bless the house. As he sprinkled holy water and continued performing the blessing he began to feel extreme cold spots. Not long into the ritual, after entering what would later be the "sewing room", he claimed he encountered huge numbers of flies, and heard a disembodied voice tell him to "Get out!". He was also forcefully slapped across the face, as if by unseen hands.

Father Ray left the house without telling the Lutzs what happened. He did tell George to make sure no one slept in that room (they agreed and made it their sewing room). In some accounts, the Lutzs had problems communicating with Father Ray. Before Ray could report any other details of what he experienced, static on the phone line grew and he was soon disconnected. From that point forward phone communication between the Lutzs in their home, and the priest was nearly impossible, as static noise on the line or disconnections eventually plagued every attempt. However, Father Ray was dealing with his own troubles.

Father Ray would reportedly develop a fever and stigmata like blisters on his hands shortly after his trip to bless the house. He mentioned this in subsequent interviews and he claimed that anytime he attempted to discuss the house and the Lutzs in his office with anyone, he would experience cold spots and other unusual phenomenon. The Lutzs reportedly reached him by phone on their last night in the house and he asked them what they were still doing there.

The Lutzs Move in and the Activity Begins

The Lutzs were excited to move into their new dream house. They had their hands full, combining two houses worth of items together with the items kept from the DeFeos, and their vehicles, including the boats in the boathouse. They also noticed the house had an unusual "deadness of sound".

Outside noises, cars driving by the front of the house, nearby street noises, animals, and other sounds didn't penetrate the house and couldn't be heard. In contrast, the family started noticing unusual sounds in the house including scraping noises, and banging noises. They relegated these sounds to merely normal for older houses or the building "settling". Shortly after the move-in, Kathy claimed to experience a sensation she described as an unseen embrace or "ethereal hug" and the scent of perfume. She attributed it to the spirit of the DeFeo mother. She described it as a reassuring embrace as if welcoming her family to the house like one mother to another

Unwelcome Christmas Presents

The Lutzs claim the unusual activity in the house started taking a darker turn shortly after Christmas (echoing Ronnie DeFeo). Large gatherings of flies were encountered in various parts of the house (something highly unusual in the winter). George Lutz would kill the flies, only to have them reappear day after day. The flies were reportedly there at move-in, but their presence and persistence began to draw more attention.

Other odd things drew the family's attention. The interiors of the ceramic toilets would frequently turn black with a strange black ichor. The key holes in many doors would become filled with a strange substance that would drip and harden. The family discovered a green gelatin like substance on carpets, and in certain parts of the house, which also came back daily. Occasionally, the crosses the Lutz family had put up on the walls would be turned upside down.

Kathy began hearing more scraping and banging noises, and even sounds that reminded her of footsteps on the floor above. George began to hear doors slamming, but upon investigating would often find the dog in front of the door in question, sound asleep. The door itself, undisturbed and locked. It wasn't just the Lutz's that experienced these bizarre situations, guests, family, and friends that came to their home reportedly encountered unusual sounds and activity, often coming from upstairs.

The Lutzs and others tried often to find logical sources for the noises. They searched for loose wires, open panels, damaged hinges, and other things, but could never find reasonable explanations. Even more unnerving perhaps, than the changes in the house over time, were the changes the family themselves were experiencing.

Disturbing Sleep Patterns and Personality Changes

The Lutzs reportedly began experiencing an odd feeling that compelled them to stay at the house and not leave. It became more pronounced as the buildup of

NEW YORK
Historic Haunts of the North II

paranormal activity increased. Further, they described feeling as if their personalities were changing. They started arguing more frequently and seemed to have short tempers. In addition, the whole family, with the exception of George, all started sleeping facedown on their stomachs (resembling the DeFeo family). George later claimed the kids started saying strange things and acting odd.

The family began having vivid nightmares. In them they experienced the DeFeo family killings firsthand, as if they were the victims themselves. These dreams would include details of the murders, such as the order of the murders, or where the bullets entered and exited the bodies. These details were never released to the general public, but when matched later to police reports of the DeFeo killings, were reportedly identical. Kathy experienced these dreams more than the others.

Meanwhile, Kathy's husband, George would find himself waking up each night around the time of the murder (3:15 a.m). Now awake, he would find himself compelled to check on the kids or to visit the boathouse (whose doors he kept discovering open). George also began experiencing a sort of bone-chilling cold, from which he couldn't warm up. He became fixated, constantly chopping wood and attempting to keep the fire burning in a feeble attempt to remove the cold sensation he was experiencing. The fire burned constantly and a strange and dark marking began to etch itself in the back of the fireplace. A mark described as demonic in appearance.

So fixated was George on keeping the fire going, that he began to forego eating, losing lots of weight in the process, and ignoring his grooming. He later described feeling as if he was becoming like Ronnie DeFeo Jr. (to whom he bore a resemblance), even sharing similar disturbing thoughts. George was not the only one affected by the house, the kids began to have their own experiences.

Missy's Playmates, and the Coming of "Jodie"

The Lutz children, like their father, began to experience their own unusual activity. Windows flew open in the boy's room and other parts of the house. Danny's hands were allegedly crushed flat one day while trying to close the window in the sewing room. The family was afraid he might lose digits. A short time later they discovered his hands were fine with barely a mark to indicate anything happened. Still, the most disturbing events were connected not to the Lutz boys, but to Melissa or "Missy" and the invisible ethereal being that identified itself as "Jodie" (or Jody).

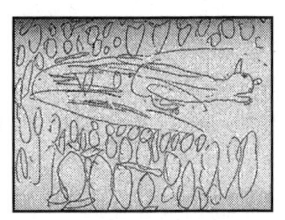

Jodie Drawing
GJ Fredbear/Amityville Wiki
Creative Commons (CC BY-SA)

Missy told her parents she had two friends she played with, one a small boy and the other, more frequent playmate, was Jodie. According to Missy, Jodie was an angel with red eyes that could change size and shape at will. It could only be seen if it wished to be seen. Jodie was depicted as a pig in the book (though Missy's drawings made it look like more of a cat). George and Kathy decided

NEW YORK

The Amityville Horror House

these were imaginary friends, and paid little attention at first.

Missy's interactions with Jodie would eventually become more sinister and too unusual to just ignore. Jodie would repeatedly make the rocking chair and other items in Missy's room move, but would stop immediately and perhaps unnaturally when her parents arrived (rocking chair stopped mid rock). Missy would often sing songs to entertain Jodie. If she was called to leave the room (for dinner or otherwise) she would cease her song at the threshold as she left. She would pick up the song upon re-entering the room from the exact spot she stopped, even if several hours had passed. Jodie told Missy that she and the Lutz family would always be there. Kathy Lutz's sister-in-law (her brother's wife) stayed with the family and alleged that she was awakened by the ghost of a sickly-looking little boy, sitting on the edge of her bed, asking where Missy and Jodie were, before vanishing into thin air! Kathy and George eventually spotted Jodie's red eyes outside of the window.

The Red Room and More Activity

After moving a bookshelf in the basement, Kathy Lutz claimed to discover a secret Red Room in the basement. The room was not part of the original plans of the house and was painted a pronounced red color. The room was supposedly much colder than the rest of the house and had a strong offensive odor. Harry, the family dog, avoided it at all costs even cowering from it if forced towards it.

While Kathy was unnerved by the sudden discovery of the Red Room, George began to have his own unsettling experiences. He awoke one evening to find his wife hovering over the bed (the boys supposedly had the same experience over their beds). On another occasion, he awoke to see his wife resembling a 90 year old woman! Kathy was shocked by her elderly appearance as well, which thankfully, faded by morning.

George also began to hear sounds coming from the living room, which he likened to a marching band warming up. No one else in the house heard it. He would frequently run down from his bedroom to a place where he thought the sounds were originating to find nothing. While the living room was typically undisturbed in appearance during these encounters, occasionally the rug and the furniture would be moved as if making room for a large group.

The Lutzs were still feeling an unnatural desire to remain in the house, despite the paranormal activity. Now certain of the activity in the house, they tried to connect with Ronnie DeFeo's attorney, William Weber, thinking there may have been something to his client's claims of paranormal activity. This decision would come to haunt them later.

Bad Blessings and the Beginning of the End

At this point the Lutzs claimed they had repeatedly been unsuccessful trying to contact Father Ray and get him back out to the house. Having no luck, they

NEW YORK

decided to move from room to room and attempt to re-bless the house themselves with a crucifix. They didn't make it very far before they heard a choir of aggravated disembodied voices forcefully exclaim "Will you please stop!" The Lutz's failed blessing apparently kicked the paranormal activity into overdrive.

The Last Night in the House

On the night of January 14, 1976 (28 days after moving in), George Lutz thought he heard a storm outside. The house suddenly became very active. The children's beds were reportedly levitated and slammed to the floor. The doors of the house sounded as if they were violently swung open and slammed shut. Sleeping just beside Kathy, George, at first, could not get out of bed to investigate. He felt as if something was holding him down and his muscles were locked. Like some unseen presence had just crawled into bed with them. The dog began to repeat his own weird activity; walking in circles, vomiting, and then going back to sleep.

Once they managed to get out of bed, the Lutzs made yet another attempt to bless the house. It went as well as the last. It was at this point that the family successfully reached out to Father Ray. They agreed to get out and Father Ray told them not to take anything. What transpired as they were leaving remains to some degree a mystery, as all involved claimed it "too frightening" to describe. What little the family mentioned, includes the fact that George spotted a hooded figure, as the family fled, similar in appearance to the diabolical image etched in the fireplace wall.

The Lutzs left the home with a minimum of clothing and none of their possessions. The motorcycles, boat, and other vehicles and items were also left in the boathouse. Fortunately for the family, George had previously installed a switch in the family van that allowed him to change from automatic starter to manual. As the family tried to make a quick exit, the car wouldn't start. George switched the car over to manual and they were able to start the vehicle and leave.

What Happened Next?

They made their way to Kathy's mother's house, the van was reportedly being rocked and beaten on by some unseen force along the way. Over the next few days the family regrouped. They were hoping to contact Hans Holzer, the most celebrated and active author/parapsychologist at the time. Unfortunately, when they reached out they discovered Holzer was unavailable (he was involved in another investigation). The Lutzs continued reaching out exploring options for help with the house and their situation.

This was the first time the family sat down and compared notes on their encounters. They discovered each family member had experienced numerous events in the house, some connected, some not. Each was surprised to learn what the others had gone through. They began to believe the house altered their perceptions in various ways. The family decided to make tapes to collect all the events and details they could recall.

George and Kathy began drinking heavily after leaving the house to help deal with what had happened. Unfortunately, they also soon learned that whatever forces had affected them at the house in Amityville had followed them. Kathy would reportedly again experience levitation with George in their temporary bedroom. The rest of the family also began encountering other paranormal activity (though thankfully, not to the level that led up to that final night).

Help is on the Way?

One of the first successful contacts the Lutzs had with someone in the parnanormal field was Stephen Kaplan, a man who claimed to be a vampirologist and parapsychologist. This was in mid February, weeks after fleeing the house. George Lutz and Kaplan discussed the idea of Kaplan investigating the Amityville House along with his associates at the Parapsychology Institute of America on Long Island (a reportedly non-profit group). Lutz inquired if there was a fee to investigate, Kaplan allegedly told him no, but that any fraudulent activity would be exposed. George's main condition to agree to investigation, was keeping details away from the press, as he feared his kids would be besieged with reporters and unwelcome attention.

Kaplan allegedly went straight to the press against the Lutz family wishes. This breach of trust, combined with some questions about the legitimacy of Kaplan's credentials, reportedly caused the family to cancel their involvement with him. However, the press had been contacted and the cat was out of the bag. This led to a press conference at William Weber's office. George, allegedly hoping to minimize the damage, and attention on the kids, reluctantly told the press he and his family had been driven out of the house by a "very strong force".

Kaplan claimed that they cancelled because they feared they'd be discovered. He became a staunch skeptic of the story, and later wrote a book called ***The Amityville Horror Conspiracy***, the rights of which were sold by Kaplan, and later formed the basis for the ***Amityville 3-D*** film. Kaplan's claims, and his book, would be disputed by the Lutzs and the couple soon to be at the center of the investigation of the house, Ed and Lorraine Warren.

The Coming of Ed and Lorraine Warren

Marvin Scott and Laura Didio, newsreporters for Channel 5 in New York were involved in connecting the Lutz family with the Warrens. Ed and Lorraine Warren had a reputation for dealing with paranormal activity. They founded the New England Society for Psychic Research (NESPR) in 1952. Ed was a self professed demonologist, Lorraine was a clairvoyant and light trance medium. It was the hope of the Lutz's that the Warrens could "cleanse" the Amityville House, "fixing it" so they could once again live there.

NEW YORK
Historic Haunts of the North II

The Warrens were deeply religious, especially Lorraine. She claimed to have had a strong feeling of apprehension after being contacted to investigate the home. She reached out to her contacts to pray with her and for the Lutz family.

Lorraine and the Miraculous Padre Pio

*Padre Pio
Public
Domain*

Lorraine Warren was a fan of Friar Padre Pio, an Italian Franciscan monk. Padre Pio was considered a mystic, who manifested the stigmata for decades. He was allegedly able to levitate, read souls, bilocate, and perform healings. He was also at the center of other preternatural phenomenon claiming at times he did combat with demons, devils and unholy minions (a claim backed by his fellow priests). Pio also allegedly had the gift of prophecy. He died in 1968, his 50 year stigmata disappeared from his body shortly after his death. He became canonized and recognized as a Saint by Pope John Paul II in 2002.

Padre Pio passed away before Lorraine Warren could meet him. However, she was given an anonymous envelope from a go-between with a rosary, a gift sent to her posthumously from Padre Pio, shortly before the Amityville investigation. She would carry it on many investigations and claimed it and he, frequently protected her from the more nefarious forces she encountered.

Investigating the Amityville House

Ed and Lorraine first visited the house on February 24, 1976. The impressions they got caused them to believe more research and a second investigation was needed. This time with help!

They began to dig deeper into the case and they reportedly met with the Lutz family at Kathy's mother's home along with Father Ray. The Warrens were often known to include a variety of individuals in their investigations presumably to get a variety of opinions, including researchers, college students, scientists, and others. The second more formal and vigorous investigation of the Amityville House would follow this same pattern.

News reporter Laura Didio from Channel 5 helped the Warrens gather credible and reputable people to include in their investigation. She was surprised to learn that George too had been reaching out trying to get help. Some 21 people were present for the second investigation on March 6, 1976. The group were hoping members of the Lutz family would join them since they had agreed to the investigation. However, George and the family wouldn't go into the house. Instead, George met the crew and interviewing team and gave them the key.

Among those on site that night were Laura Didio and Marvin Scott from Channel 5, Michael Linder, a radio reporter, numerous cameramen including Steve Petropolis (for Channel 5), and Gene Campbell, a professional photographer that had worked with the Warrens. Among the academics present were researchers from Duke University, paranormal investigators Paul Bartz, George Kekoris, Jerry Solfvin (investigator for The Psychical Research Foundation in Durham), Dr. Alice Tanous, Dr. Karl Osis (both members of The American Society of Psychical Research Manhattan), as well as Dr. Brian Riley. Alberta Riley (Brian's wife, and a psychic medium) was also present, as were other psychics and sensitives, including Mary Downey, Mary Pascarella, and of course Lorraine Warren. Ed Warren served as the defacto head of the investigation.

From the onset, there was unusual activity. The investigating team reportedly discovered the dripping and hardened substances still coming out of the key holes on the doors (especially from the second floor). Ed went to the basement with a crucifix. As he walked around, he reportedly felt a pressure as if he was being pushed to the ground. He claimed it became hard to breathe and he felt pinpricks like electricity.

Meanwhile upstairs, Lorraine began to feel very uncomfortable. She felt an overwhelming sense of sadness and depression. She also picked up on the presence of menacing and unnatural energies in the house. Like Ed, she felt a pressure on her and she also picked up on another undisclosed or unreleased police detail. The DeFeo family's bodies were lined up in the front facing room of the house on the bottom floor before being taken to the morgue.

A cameraman who had never been to the house before or examined its floorplan received a flash of insight on the steps. He turned and relayed to his companions from the first few steps the exact layout of the second floor. As he ventured farther up the stairs he too felt pressure on his chest and almost fell backwards. He suffered heart palpitations and had to be assisted. Other camera crew members reportedly collapsed, and a Duke reporter was reportedly tossed backward in his chair by some sort of paranormal force.

The decision was made to hold a séance (depicted somewhat in the beginning of the film *The Conjuring II*), a decision Lorraine later claimed was a bad idea. Laura Didio would later describe watching some of the psychics present get violently ill, and other odd behaviors exhibited by them with the crew. Lorraine and the psychics felt that Ronnie DeFeo Jr. may have dabbled in the "Black Arts" in the Red Room.

Many of the psychics present that night were so badly affected by what they came into contact with, that they left the paranormal field altogether! Mary Pascarella, a practicing Catholic, who once investigated phenomenon for the Archdiocese of Bridgeport, was so upset with whatever she made contact with, that she stopped doing investigations and moved out of state, and cross country. Lorraine connected on some level with malevolent forces and was convinced that she wouldn't have made it through without the help of the crucifix and the assistance of Padre Pio's spirit.

The presence of spirits, and Lorraine's claims of protection from them, were confirmed perhaps by two unusual photographs captured that night by automatic

NEW YORK
Historic Haunts of the North II

cameras. The first a photo containing an apparent image of Padre Pio that seemed to appear in one of the rooms when Lorraine felt most under attack and asked for his help. The second photo was of a ghost boy with glowing eyes that resembled the murdered boy John DeFeo (there were no children in the house that night). The Lutz's daughter Missy would later say that the ghost boy depicted in the photo looked like the spirit she and Jodie used to play with.

The Menacing Aftermath

After the cameras stopped rolling, and the team went their separate ways (some never to return to the field) the Warrens went home. Shortly after they arrived, Ed went to his workshop at the opposite end of the house, while Lorraine remained in the bedroom. The Warrens claimed the entities from the house followed them and attacked them that night. Ed described a sort of tornado of malevolent energy that he barely managed to drive away with faith, the cross, and holy water. Meanwhile, Lorraine claimed her faith in Padre Pio again helped her drive the diabolical forces away.

Lorraine would later describe the Amityville case as her worst ever, and the most disturbing. She claimed she levitated while in the house and was directly affected by other unseen forces. George Lutz would later suggest in an interview with her that perhaps the house felt the Warrens were a threat.

The Lutzs Shortly after the Investigation

The Warrens had retrieved some pieces of paperwork for the Lutz family while in the house, and the Lutzs tried to stick to Father Ray's advice and leave most of the stuff there. George had a few items he wanted though, chief among them, a chest made by his grandfather that contained family pictures. He asked a few friends to go in the house and get it, along with a few other small things. The friends agreed and went to the house on Easter Sunday, April 18th (perhaps thinking the holy quality of the day might protect them). All non-believers, they drank in the house, and laughed about it all. They didn't experience anything unusual. However, one of those friends was reportedly murdered by his girlfriend a week later (a coincidence perhaps).

Meanwhile, the Lutzs were still experiencing activity at Kathy's mother's house. Kathy even reportedly turned again into the old crone, this time her mother was a witness to it as well. The Lutzs would reportedly continue experiencing paranormal activity for years.

Other investigators claimed they could cleanse the house, and the Lutzs held out hope. Unfortunately, the others ultimately proved unsuccessful or unreliable. Eventually, the Lutzs had everything auctioned off or given away, even the canned food in the kitchen, and the van they escaped in. They gave the house back to the bank. In an effort to get as far away as they could from the house and the situation, and perhaps get some relief, they would move to California.

NEW YORK
The Amityville Horror House

Ronnie DeFeo's attorney William Weber was interested in making a book with them from their story. They were interested as well, until they looked over the contract and discovered murderer Ronnie DeFeo would get part of the profits, and that there were several clauses in the contract that gave Weber authority over how and to whom, the story was told moving forward. It also reportedly included several loopholes that would give Weber the house and exclude the Lutzs. Not wanting Ronnie to profit off the murders, and citing the other unfriendly clauses in the contract, they reportedly declined.

Instead, they were put in touch (through another friend) with a publishing house Prentice-Hall, and author Jay Anson. Anson had reportedly been involved in documentaries. The Lutzs thought he'd write a truthful account. Hoping to have a book made, but not wanting to relive their experiences, they handed the tapes they had made earlier over to Anson, along with materials they collected from the Amityville Historical Society. Anson would do his own research, interview others, and include additional material while writing what would become a best selling novel.

William Weber, in the meantime, put plans in motion for an article about the house, an apparent "hit piece" that appeared in **Good Housekeeping**. He claimed the story was a hoax made up by himself with Anson and the Lutzs over wine (like his client DeFeo, his story would change with retellings). However, in direct contrast to the claim, he arranged to have the bank (who now owned the house) allow him to bring in Hans Holzer to investigate. Interestingly, the author of the article in Good Housekeeping was the person Weber reportedly originally picked to write the book about the house and the Lutzs. His motives and story came under further scrutiny when it was discovered he was in the middle of a lawsuit with the Lutzs. A judge even called him out for acting less like a lawyer for his client, and more like a literary agent.

Hans Holzer's Amityville Investigation

Hans Holzer investigated the Amityville house on January 13, 1977, with psychic Ethel Johnson and reporter Laura Didio. Holzer's team had trouble with some of their equipment (which worked perfectly after they left). Hans Holzer and his team used their equipment to take photographs at the scene. These photos revealed curious anomalies, including halos which appeared in the supposed images of bullet marks made in the original 1974 murders.

parapsychologist Hans Holzer Public Domain Image

Ethel had never been to the home and was unfamiliar with the house and the details of the case. However, she immediately picked up on and described Ronnie DeFeo's actions on that fateful night. Ethel also picked up on spiritual activity and a Native American connection. She claimed, "Whoever lives here is going to

75

NEW YORK

Historic Haunts of the North II

be the victim of all the anger…the blind fierceness…"

Holzer came to the same conclusion that the Lutz's and Warren's did, that there were malevolent forces at work in the house. Ethel claimed an angry Native American chief was behind the hauntings, and had possessed Ronnie DeFeo Jr. Holzer would use these details along with his own research and conclusions to write **Murder in Amityville**, along with Weber. He would later write two more books on the subject, *The Amityville Curse*, and *The Secret of Amityville*. Like several others, he claimed the site had tie-ins to nearby Native American tribes and like the other books, Holzer's would later be used to make other Amityville films.

The Amityville Horror Book and Movie

Jay Anson completed his book, and the galleys were sent to the Lutzs to look over. This was reportedly the first time they learned of Father Ray's experiences outside and inside the house (he would confirm some of these details when interviewed anonymously on the program *In Search Of*). They noticed other details they hadn't been familiar with and some discrepancies in the book, but more than likely attributed them to artistic license. They signed a book deal shortly before the book's release in 1977. They received some cash advances on the book, but ended up spending most of it defending their story and the rights to it over the next several years. They were eventually given sequel rights, and hoped to re-interview everyone involved and work with an author to create another version of the story. This time they hoped to create a story that was more factual and didn't have all the improvised Hollywood details and additions.

The Amityville Horror
Author's Collection

After the success of Jay Anson's book, the decision was made to make a movie version. The town of Amityville, however, wanted nothing to do with it! The non-stop cascade of interested tourists, paranormal investigators, crackpots, and others had driven the town and the residents of the street to the breaking point. No filming was allowed. Instead, the film company had to recreate the now infamous house elsewhere (in New Jersey), and the film was shot away from Amityville.

To a movie going public eagerly awaiting these type of horror movies (especially since the release of *The Exorcist* earlier in the decade), it was a huge smash. It earned Jay Anson and the movie company millions while leaving the Lutzs with a small fraction of that and with even more problems. The inconsistencies in the book, and further changes to the story when given the "Hollywood treatment" (exploding windows and doors, etc.) created even more controversy and claims that the story was a hoax. Even Hans Holzer acknowledged the Lutz's story in the book had been, "…embellished, enlarged and elaborated upon…"

NEW YORK
The Amityville Horror House

The Lutz Family After the Movie Goes from Bad to Worse.

The Lutzs would find themselves in the middle of a storm. Over the following years, George and Kathy would take three different sets of lie detector tests and voice stress tests administered by some of the best and most respected members of their fields. They would pass them all, even when those administering the tests included questions about levitation and other paranormal instances mentioned in their story (and frequently called into question by skeptics). Their answers even seemed to convince the examiners, who started wearing their crucifixes and going to church again. Despite this, the Lutzes were repeatedly forced to defend themselves in other interviews and in court, where movie companies made more outlandish sequels from Holzer's books, Kaplan's books, and others. They were again excluded and forced to fight for their rights to the story they lived through; 13 years of lawsuits followed.

The Lutz family claimed in the aftermath of the experiences they went through, that they became deeply religious (George and Kathy both reportedly entered the ministry). That didn't help much on the paranormal front, as they were still experiencing intermittent periods of intense activity. "Jodie" even allegedly followed the family to California. The process of Missy having to tell Jodie to go away caused more activity and situations that the family again felt uncomfortable discussing. In fact, the paranormal activity only diminished years later, when after years of asking for help, the Lutzs were blessed by an agent of the Archbishop of Canterbury.

The Lutzs would have two more children after Amityville, both girls Like their parents, three of their kids would also enter the ministry. The boys would each have issues with George as they grew up and separated themselves. The Lutzs would ultimately end up divorced. Kathy Lutz would die of emphysema August 17, 2004. George would pass a few years later, on May 8, 2006, of heart disease. Their deaths involved nothing suspicious or eerie. Both fervently maintained until the end, that their story was mostly true and that the hauntings happened.

As a matter of fact, no Lutz family member ever claimed the situation was a hoax. The Lutz sons (now adults), vehemently claim the hauntings were real. Chris confirmed in interviews that the supernatural forces at play followed the family to his grandmother's house and to California. He claims he and his brother shared the infamous room with the half moon, eye-like windows, and had encounters there as well as in other parts of the house. Like George, he saw the strange hooded figure in the house. He admits the books and movies exaggerated the details. (windows often flew open, but were not blown out like they were in the movies for example). Chris also stated that there were a few inaccurate claims (like doors ripping off their hinges). He claims his stepfather George brought trouble on the family while dabbling in the occult inside the house.

Daniel, his brother, also believed George's attempts to dabble in the occult were

NEW YORK
Historic Haunts of the North II

to blame for the activity. He would go on to participate in a documentary, *My Amityville Horror*. In that piece he also claimed that George demonstrated telekinetic abilities and that he and George experienced "bodily possession". He states that the story, the whole situation, and defending the story against claims of a hoax, has ruined his life.

Both boys recognize that the book's details are wildly exaggerated in many instances (like the exploding windows). They say that George Lutz was not the "innocent victim" or "family savior" seen in the book and movie. In fact, they continue to claim it was George Lutz's tapping into dark forces that started the trouble. They suggest that their mother went along with many things regarding the book at George's forceful insistence. They also seem to suggest that George reaching out for help in the paranormal community, was akin to trying to call in the cavalry after you've gotten in way over your head.

Still, they confirmed many of the frightening details in the book, including their beds levitating, the swarming flies, black toilets, and more. According to them George only stopped dabbling in dark things after his experiences in the house, and after Father Ray told him to stop. However, whatever George conjured up was attached to them and continues to plague them. Some of it stopped with the blessing the Lutz's received, but the boys at least, have alluded to the fact that they've been dealing with dark forces since. They are apparently reluctant to discuss it because of the media circus surrounding all of it, and those that would be eager to grab any other details to exploit in further books and movies (there are several in the works and most are pure speculative fiction).

They call out those that claim that Amityville was a complete hoax. They point out (rightly so) that most skeptics were never part of the investigations or in some cases even alive at the time! These skeptics and naysayers stood to make money from books, movies, podcasts, and more on the topic (they did and still do). They also claim many of the details the skeptics jump on (the family's financial troubles, etc.) were also exaggerated or falsely represented.

Reporter Laura Didio was also involved in the *My Amityville Horror* documentary. She verified unusual behavior on the part of the psychics and sensitives in the house, during the Warren's second investigation. She reiterated that as a reporter who could not see the spectral forces at work, and wasn't present for some of Warren's reported encounters, she couldn't confirm the house's haunted status. However, she did claim while working with Holzer, to see an adam's apple form on the neck of Holzer's female psychic as she was channeling a male spirit guide in the Amityville house! She also said she interviewed a later resident of the house who was very personable in general conversation, until asked about the haunts in the house. At that moment

The Amityville House circa 2005
Public Domain Image

the host eerily snapped her kneck around to stare at Didio and claimed there was nothing here until George and Danny summoned it.

"The Amityville Hoax" Considered

The accusations that the Amityville haunting was a hoax began almost as soon as the news of the case broke. Fueled no doubt, by Ronnie DeFeo's lawyer William Weber and his accusations of concocting the story. Unfortunately for them, the Lutzs did discuss the idea of their story becoming a book with Weber and it was recorded on tape. Still, there are several other factors skeptics point to when calling this story a hoax.

First and most prevalent, residents and owners of the house at 112 Ocean Avenue after the Lutz's, beginning with the Cromartie family, and continuing to this day, have publicly claimed no paranormal activity in the house. In fact, they claim the only unusual activity is the nonstop barrage of people drawn to the house and the area by the stories. They site instances of break-ins, vandalism, and other uncomfortable situations.

The owners and locals, dislike how the media and Hollywood have drawn so much attention to the house, the town, and shed such a negative light on the whole area. I don't blame them! More recent owners have done everything they can to deter the zealous fan base, from re-numbering the house, to making cosmetic changes to the house to make it less recognizable (like removing the iconic half moon windows). The house has sold several times over the last few years, most likely due more to the negative attention and rabid fans, than to ghosts.

It's worth noting, however, both the Lutzs and the Warrens have detailed in interviews that whatever supernatural forces may have been present in the house, followed the family to other locations. This begs the obvious question, could whatever was at work in the house have simply left, attached to the Lutzs? This would explain the lack of reported activity by subsequent owners.

Addressing this directly in his books, Ed Warren claims the Cromarties bought the house hoping they'd make a fortune from the film company using it to make the movie. When that fell through, they attempted to convince everyone it was a hoax to drive the curiosity seekers and others away. Warren claimed there was some unusual activity that continued in or around the house (like their car catching fire, and Barbara Cromartie's son possibly dying there of a drug overdose), but the family covered it up.

The owners of the home since the Moynahans have all experienced dramatic life changing events, including losing businesses, divorces (for the majority of the owners), and obviously death in the case of the DeFeos. The Warren's nephew John Zaffis, also a storied paranormal investigator, author, and demonologist, claims in interviews that it's pretty common for occupants of homes with bad auras to have money issues, divorce, and other problems. He also felt—like the Warrens—that there may have been a buildup of psychic and paranormal energy

79

NEW YORK
Historic Haunts of the North II

in the house that just needed the right occupants to surge and release, and the Lutzs were the unfortunate family to experience it.

Another thing working against the Lutzs' story and in favor of the skeptics, are some of the details of the story itself. While it's not unusual for movies to change the name of real people involved (like Father Ray who became Father Delaney in the film), the car Ray drove was changed, and many of the details of the story were exaggerated or fabricated (most likely by the Hollywood filmmakers and screenwriters). Skeptics insist the Lutzs changed the details for a better story, and that these details are simply impossible to believe. The Warrens addressed this by indicating that people present in a paranormally active site can experience a sort of "telepathic hypnosis", making people see things through their mind's eye that aren't actually there, but appear real, presumably to scare them more (like bleeding walls or doors blown off their hinges).

Unfortunately, the Warren's details of the event and their interviews became fodder for skeptics as well. As the Warrens, and Lutzs were subject to all manner of questions and repeated interviews over the years, at times their details in their stories, and their answers changed somewhat. Especially the interviews in their later years (closer to the times of their passing). Skeptics examined details like the weather (with weather bureau experts) recorded during the Lutz's occupation in the house, and stated it was impossible for the Lutzs to have seen Jodie's cloven footprints in the snow leading to the boathouse and dock, since there was no snow that day! Nor was there a storm on the final night according to them. In addition, they claim Father Ray was never swarmed by flies, and that even he changed his story somewhat under a legal affidavit. He was also, to some degree, allegedly prevented from discussing details by the church. He ultimately left the state and changed professions.

Some of the skeptics have solid points. The Lutz family has admitted in interviews, there was some exaggeration. Hollywood has a reputation for taking the license to alter stories to make for more provocative movies. This was certainly true in this case. Unfortunately, even before the movie was made. Jay Anson and his editors took several artistic liberties in the book it was based on.

First, they called the book a "true story" hoping to generate more sensationalism about it and beef up sales (it worked). This alone would invite meticulous scrutiny. However, they also changed some of the dates of the events in the book. This has brought additional heat on everyone involved. Skeptics keenly pouring over details noted the discrepancies in the accounts created because of these changes. Believers would counter with the idea that Hollywood and writers always take artistic license with stories. They would also point out that older people often fail to recall exact details, or match stories perfectly during follow up tellings. Still, those discrepancies fed the fire of skeptics and do so to this day.

Adding to the problem, the publishers of most of the other books about the case, like Anson, (follow ups by authors like John Jones, who had more direct involvement with the Lutz family), were supposed to list those books as "fiction based on fact", instead, they were again often categorized as nonfiction in the hopes of drawing more readers and selling more books. This meant the details of these stories also came under closer scrutiny.

Some of the skeptics have even interviewed Ed and Lorraine Warren themselves, and called Lorraine's claims of extrasensory abilities into question. Especially after more recent remakes of the Amityville film and the other connected Conjuring films. These stories bring more apparent discrepancies, or perhaps more instances of artistic license in the production.

To quiet critics, Lorraine had her abilities tested by Dr. Thelma Moss in a UCLA lab. Dr. Moss found Lorraine's clairvoyance was "far above average". Respected reporter Laura Didio also mentioned in interviews that she was frequently an eyewitness to paranormal activity in some of the Warren's cases. Skeptics claim the Warren's approach should have been more scientific and precise, the Warrens feel the skeptics fail to acknowledge the part religion played in the case.

Obviously many of the skeptics, like Kaplan and others, had personal reasons for proving the story was a hoax. While Kaplan had pre-investigation involvement with the case, others (who didn't) have been embroiled in lawsuits with the Lutzs over the details and tellings. In most cases, these skeptics stood to significantly profit financially from their books and possible movies (and did).

Responding to the critics, the Warrens themselves offered a sizable cash reward for anyone who would come forward and debate with them on air and prove Amityville was a hoax. There were no takers. Kaplan in particular, was scheduled to do so several times, but was a frequent no show. According to my research, none of the skeptics who've written about the investigation and reviewed the facts of the case were actually present at the Warren's or Holzer's investigations. I always get a kick out of those that didn't participate in a complicated situation originally, but come along after the fact, when all the witnesses are gone, and much of the evidence cold, and claim to quickly have the definitive version of the story. Often, they claim that the answer is that it never happened. However, in my experiences the truth tends to lie somewhere in the middle. The Lutz family as I mentioned earlier, have stuck to their claims of paranormal activity in the house, as have the Warrens and those present at the investigations.

Some Additional Eyebrow Raising Details

Lorraine began her career as a noted skeptic. It was only after multiple cases and encounters with Ed that she changed her mind. It's ironic that she would end up being the target of so many skeptics.

Malachi Martin, a high ranking priest in the Catholic Church, has become the subject of much controversy over the last few years. He claims the Catholic Church knew the house at Amityville was haunted despite their official stance. It

NEW YORK
Historic Haunts of the North II

is a claim he has made repeatedly in interviews, and his unique position in the church would have allowed him to have access to this information.

While writing ***The Amityville Horror*** and a follow up book, author Jay Anson experienced some "high-strangeness" of his own. He gave a good friend the first few chapters of what would become ***The Amityville Horror*** to take home and read. That night she was killed in a fire with her two daughters. Anson's editor's car caught fire after taking a copy of the book back to the publisher's office. Anson's follow up book was titled 666. He died of a heart attack shortly after finishing the final chapter in the story.

Heart problems seem to be a common issue in relation to the Amityville story. All the men present at the Warren's investigation died from or experienced severe heart attacks or heart issues. Ed Warren also learned while researching the case that his mother passed away at the exact moment of the DeFeo murders.

Unable to shoot in Amityville, Toms River New Jersey was the place where the filmmakers recreated the De Feo/Lutz house for the movie. The movie makers blew up the house and rebuilt a new one on site. Like the original, it has drawn enormous groups of visitors and attention. Like the original, its appearance has since been altered to detract this attention. Like the original, there are several reports that would seem to indicate it's haunted!

As mentioned, in the years following the original events, the Warrens and Lutzs have been interviewed numerous times. In several cases, the radio station, TV station, podcasters, and others have experienced unusual technical difficulties and broadcast problems while trying to interview and record them. In some cases, these technical difficulties resemble the static effects and disconnects the Lutz family reportedly had while trying to contact Father Ray. In other cases, significant parts of an entire week of broadcasts (dedicated to getting all the details out) were cut short or canceled due to these difficulties.

The Lutz sons, for the longest time, had avoided the house and discussing the case. On at least one occasion, one of the boys, now grown, stopped in front of the house in the wee hours and proceeded to loudly vent his aggravation against the house and the situation. He then returned home. In the days that followed, he reportedly found himself plagued by a sudden onslaught of paranormal activity!

Riddle Me This

If William Weber truly concocted the story with Anson, and or the Lutz's help, then why require them to take a lie detector test in their contract. Also why go back and investigate with Hans Holzer. Weber obviously wanted his own books.

Further, if the Lutzs were perpetuating a hoax, why wouldn't they retrieve their belongings which are fairly unimportant to the story? More importantly, why not retrieve their expensive vehicles from the boathouse (as they didn't play as big of a part in the story)? Why allow it all to be sold at auction for a big loss (especially if they had financial issues as some skeptics claim)? If the Lutzs were as strapped for cash as they say, then why did the Lutzs pay several months on the house after they left it, in the hopes that the Warrens or others might be able to cleanse the house and they could move back in. If they were broke, they could have given it back to the bank immediately after they left and saved quite a bit of money.

It's worth noting that the Lutz family also had no guarantee that Anson's book would sell like it did or that the story would be made into a movie. It seems unlikely that a newlywed couple with three additional mouths to feed would risk that, and the roof over their heads for such a big gamble (not to mention George's family surveying business and the attention this brought to their kids). Numerous friends and family who confirmed experiences of their own would also have had to be in on this, and that seems highly unlikely.

Trying to Piece Things Together about the Land, the Murders and the Hauntings.

As I mentioned originally, the Amityville case, including the extent of involvement of the Lutzs and the Warrens, is arguably the most controversial paranormal case in existence. I have researched this case off and on since I first read the book over 25 years ago. For years I've been trying to sort the truth from fiction, legends from lies, and useful from just plain crazy. I have contacted the Historical Society about the history of the area, and the property and received no help. I've contacted the local library in Amityville, and received no help. I've even sorted through things like tax and land records, and contacted the police department. Without fail, with every one of my attempts, I've received no help and no answers from anyone close to the situation. In some cases, documents seem to have been misplaced. Amityville and its residents seem determined to put this behind them despite the best efforts of Hollywood to continue to capitalize on it (and the skeptics as well).

Even those who are willing to discuss the case seem to provide contradictory accounts. Many years ago, I met someone who claimed to have a story to tell me. From this man (a supposed friend of residents that once lived in the house at 112 Ocean Avenue), I heard a second-hand account. He was a teenager at the time, and he asked his good friend (who lived in the house with his parents) if the place was haunted. He was told they never experienced anything weird and they lived there for years. The only thing weird they ever experienced was the "weirdos" knocking on their door, trying to get in or trying desperately to take pictures of their house. They eventually moved because they got tired of the "ghost hunters".

I've also been approached at one of my book signings by a seemingly credible gentleman asking if I'd ever written anything about the Amityville House. I told him I was considering putting it in my ***Historic Haunts of the North*** books. He also claimed to know a past resident of the home, and said he'd been in the place himself. In his account, he described weird things happening all the time in the place, from things turning on and off on their own, to feelings of being watched,

83

NEW YORK
Historic Haunts of the North II

and a residence that seemed to have a distinct dislike for religious items. It's remarkably hard to get to the bottom of this story or know who to believe.

Do I believe Ronnie DeFeo was possessed? I honestly don't know. I think he was an admitted drug user, likely on a drug trip. I think something in the house may have influenced him. That is quite possible. There were too many weird things that took place that night, and prior to the murders.

It's still surprising to think no one inside or out heard the gunshots during the DeFeo murders? Paranormal situations are often marked by strange circumstances like people hearing things or seeing things that aren't physically there. However, seldom have I heard of witnesses not hearing loud things that are in close proximity (especially repeated gun shots). It's worth mentioning that the building was thought to have a high EMF reading, which is believed to sometimes cause problems with people's perceptions.

To this day many believe that the house could truly be haunted. If not by something sinister, than by the DeFeo family, murdered so horrifically in 1974. If so, it's quite possible that the family's souls are still there and looking for peace. I've never had the opportunity to see the house on Ocean Avenue for myself. It is my hope that if the DeFeo family's spirits are still lingering here, that they can move on into the light and find their peace.

Do I think the house is haunted? Not now, but possibly at one time, yes. Could whatever was here have moved on? We may never know what or who it was, but it seems to be gone. Could it have followed the Lutzs? Possibly, since they described additional strange experiences after they moved and this is not an uncommon occurence. Unfortunately, all we have now is Anson's original book, the interviews with the Warrens, the accounts of the Lutzs, the speculative writings of those who came after, and what Hollywood has sensationalized. The main players in this drama, the DeFeo family, the Warrens, and George and Kathy Lutz are all dead, only their children remain.

This is a famous house, a Historic Haunt, no doubt about it, but also a private residence. To the people of the town and the current owners, I wish you all calm, happiness, and some measure of privacy. I ask my readers to keep their inquiries simple (a quick passing photo perhaps), please let the owners and the town be. The last thing they need is mass groups of thrill seekers, on-lookers, or ghost hunters prowling their property. That being said, I believe the Warrens encountered something and I believe the Lutzs did as well. Do I believe Hollywood's version? Heavens no! In this case as in so many others, all you can do is try to research the facts and try to come up with your own conclusions.

NEW YORK

APPARITIONS AND PARANORMAL ACTIVITY AT THE ANSONIA

The Ansonia, New York City, New York

It's no surprise that as big of a city as New York is, there are numerous reports of paranormal activity and haunted locations. In fact, some in the paranormal field claim the city is the most haunted, based on the number of reported incidents and occurrences. While this may sound like an intro to a new **Ghost Busters** movie, a population this large is bound to have ghostly accounts.

One location in town which would seem to support this theory is The Ansonia. Located on the upper west side of town between West 73rd and West 74th Street; this landmark building was once billed as the grandest hotel in Manhattan. Over the years it has experienced its share of scandals, celebrities, and odd occurrences. Perhaps that's why many New Yorkers know it to be one of the most haunted spots in the city.

The Ansonia circa 1905
Public Domain

Building the Ansonia

The Ansonia was originally built as a hotel between 1899 – 1904 by William Earl Dodge Stokes (he was the Phelps – Dodge copper heir and shareholder in the Ansonia Clock Company). The hotel was named after his grandfather Anson Green Phelps, who was a well-known industrialist. Paul E. Dubsy was the architect/sculptor on the building. It was called a residential hotel which meant living there was more like apartment living. The hotel consisted of tea rooms, restaurants, ballrooms, and a beautiful fountain in the lobby that housed live seals. It was the first air-conditioned hotel in the city which made it a hot commodity (no pun intended).

The hotel also boasted elaborate external decorations, majestic gargoyles, and pneumatic tubes built into the walls that relayed messages between staff and tenants, and delivered mail underground. There were over 3000 rooms, most contained high ceilings, elegant molding, and rich details. Smaller units had no kitchens, but it didn't matter. There was a central kitchen and serving kitchens on each floor. Residents were provided the services of professional

85

NEW YORK
Historic Haunts of the North II

chefs and encouraged to dine in their apartments. The hotel had everything; even a small farm which was located on the roof.

The farm on the roof-located next to Stokes personal apartment-boasted 50 dairy cows (brought up by the cattle elevator), almost 500 chickens, goats, ducks and other animals. Every day bellhops would deliver fresh eggs to tenants (surplus was sold in the basement). Stokes goal was to make the hotel a model of early self sufficiency. The city didn't fully agree with this plan. In 1907, the health department shut the farm down

The loss of the farm didn't affect the hotel much. Its grand stylings and bohemian qualities drew celebrities, artists, musicians, athletes, and many others to move here. Over the years its residents included baseball player Babe Ruth, composer Igor Stravinsky, Italian tenor Enrico Caruso, athlete Jack Dempsey, and actors Angelina Jolie, Macaulay Culkin and Natalie Portman. The building obviously saw its share of note-worthies, but also saw its share of scandals.

Scandals at The Ansonia

As the hotel's reputation grew, it also became the site of several famous scandals. Paul Emile Dubsey, the sculptor and architect responsible for the buildings appearance, ended up in an insane asylum. Chuck Candil met here at his home with his Chicago White Sox teammates planning the notorious Black Sox Scandal. In 1930, Willie Sutton, a famous bank robber was arrested while having breakfast at the child's restaurant at The Ansonia. People were also arrested here in connection to a blackmail plot involving the Glemby jewels taken in a 1932 Robbery.

The Ansonia's Fortunes Change

With the onset of World War II, The Ansonia saw its much celebrated exterior metal decorations melted down to make tanks and bullets for the war effort. The pipes and pneumatic tubes were ripped out for similar war support efforts and the skylights were painted over. Some of the hotels most famous features were now gone.

After Stokes died, ownership slipped to a crooked landlord. The landlord would end up in jail. The building was then sold to Jake Starr, a Broadway signs manufacturer who found out it had no certificate of occupancy and thus had been operating illegally for years and millions would be needed to bring it to code. Starr began a debate in 1960 to demolish the building and build a skyscraper, but was fought off by the combined efforts of the building's artistic residents. Interestingly enough, as reports of paranormal activity increased at the hotel, it became more well known, which turned some would be residents away, but drew others.

In the 1970s The Ansonia begin to draw mediums, fortune tellers, and psychics to live, (no doubt spurred by reports of paranormal activity in the place). The Ansonia also saw a new incarnation as the Continental Bath House. Bette Midler performed here early in her career accompanied by Barry Manilow (supposedly clad only in a bath towel). The Continental Bath House's reputation grew, aided by it reportedly having the world's largest indoor pool. By the late 1970s and early 1980s, the Continental Bath House had been turned into Plato's Retreat, a reputed "sex club".

In 1992 the Ansonia was converted into condominium apartments consisting of 430 units. Many people look at the photos of this historic grand lady and wonder why it looks familiar. Besides being featured in numerous movies, the 2012 short lived network show **666 Park Avenue** used the place for exterior shots of its building, "The Drake".

More recently, a group of investors purchase the property. It took over 21 million to bring the place up to city standards for new buyers. Many have purchased space and recombined rooms in an effort to recapture the look of the original grand apartments. New buyers are also required to be told of the building's haunted status (full disclosure required by 1991 New York Supreme Court Decision). Most of these new buyers then learn what New Yorkers have known for some time, The Ansonia is very haunted.

The Haunted Ansonia

There seems to be a lot of residual energy at the Ansonia. Several residents, employees, and guests have reported many of the same occurrences. Voices are often heard in the common areas and in the hallways, shadow figures are reported there as well. Footsteps are heard so often throughout the lobby that it's practically ignored today. Things in the offices and in some of the apartments seem to disappear only to reappear in the strangest locations.

There are numerous reports of apparitions encountered throughout the hotel, (especially the basement). Many claim the place has a very haunted elevator. Most residents believe the paranormal activity is tied to an early event in the building's history.

Raising the Dead?

There is often repeated legend at The Ansonia describing a supernatural event. Onlookers at the building claim a demented doctor in a chapel connected to the hotel lobby conjured a dead person back to life. Members of building's staff claim this was the start of the paranormal activity here. I did some digging, but was unable to corroborate this unusual claim.

Regardless, reports of paranormal activity persist in the building to this day. Based on my research, nothing at The Ansonia seems to be malicious, just a little playful and perhaps in need of attention. This building to me is one of the most architecturally beautiful Historic Haunts in New York City.

NEW YORK
Historic Haunts of the North II

THE GOBLINS, GHOSTS, AND HISTORY OF BANNERMAN CASTLE

Bannerman Castle, Pollepel Island (Bannerman Island), New York

"No one can tell what associations and incidents will involve the island in the future. Time, the elements, and maybe even the goblins of the island will take their toll of some of the turrets and towers, and perhaps eventually the castle itself, but the little island will always have its place in history and in legend and will be forever a jewel in its Hudson Highland setting."
— Charles Bannerman, grandson of Francis Bannerman, in a pamphlet about the island

Bannerman Castle Courtesy Jim Sugrue

Approximately 50 miles north of New York City, not far from West Point Military Academy, lies an island in the Hudson River between Duchess and Orange County. This island is officially called Pollepel Island, but to many it's more commonly known as "Bannerman Island". Francis Bannerman, an innovative thinker, had a structure built here, uncommon to America, a castle. This "castle" is a one-of-a-kind precious gem in the Hudson Highlands area (a treasure that is unfortunately slowly crumbling and decaying). This structure, and the island it rests on, have an unusual history, and according to many, more than a few connected haunts.

The History of Pollepel Island

Long before the founding of America, this island was known to the Dutch and to Native Americans. Native American tribes believed the island was haunted and avoided it. For that reason, many people hoping to escape from Native Americans fled to this island. Once only accessible by boat, Dutch Traders and Sailors also believed there were similar forces on the island, including Goblins. The name is thought to be derived from a Dutch word for

NEW YORK
Bannerman Castle

a pit ladle or wooden spoon, and more importantly the large spoon-like contraption that would be used at times to scoop up and deposit misbehaving sailors on the island in punishment. The other suggestion for the origin of the Island's name ties into the legend of Polly Pell.

The Perils of Polly Pell

According to legend, a young woman named Polly Pell was stranded on the island in our country's infancy. While attempting to escape, she was trapped along with a companion of hers, in a segment of the frozen, but quickly breaking river ice. She was rescued by a kindly man, whom she would later marry. Whether the legend is true or not, the name Pollepel Island was already on the nautical charts by the time of the American Revolution.

The Island During the Revolutionary War and Beyond

The Hudson River was an important area to our early colonial ancestors. They hoped to defend the Hudson Highlands from the British. To that end, they put in a system of sunken logs and wooden structures all fitted with pointed metal rods designed to wreak havoc on the hulls of unsuspecting ships (termed friesian horses). These situated around the Hudson and near Pollepel Island. Unfortunately, the British figured it out soon enough, and started using flat-bottomed boats to travel the waterway. George Washington would later reportedly sign off on a plan to make Pollepel Island a military prison, but it was never built.

After the Revolutionary War, as time passed, the island had little to distinguish it in terms of inhabitants or history. It was sold to politician William Van Wyck. It was later sold to Mary G. Taft. The Taft family would eventually sell the island to the man who give it its nickname, Francis Bannerman.

The Resourceful Francis Bannerman

Francis Bannerman
Public Domain

The story of Francis Bannerman begins in a sense with his last name. Bannerman was a name derived from the sole surviving male member of the MacDonald Clan who fled slaughter at the hands of the Campbell Clan in the Glencoe Massacre. He salvaged the MacDonald Family Banner, and fled to the nearby mountains. Alluding to this, the lone survivor changed his name to Bannerman.

Francis Bannerman, a descendant, was born in Dundee, Scotland in 1851. His story reads like a real rags-to-riches tale. He came to live in America in 1854 (Brooklyn) at the age of 3. Bannerman's father was in the scrap and salvage business, and sold flags, ropes, and other items from Navy Auctions. Like his father, and his

89

NEW YORK
Historic Haunts of the North II

ancestor, he would have great success salvaging. In this case he salvaged from the Hudson Bay in a boat. He fished out old ropes, chains, and nautical items, often shed by boats along the Hudson and resting on the bottom of the River. These he resold. He discovered this could be a good source of income.

Bannerman's father left to join the Navy and fight for the North in the Civil War. Young Francis was forced to quit school and support the family in the family business. After the Civil War he found that selling old military equipment and arms could be a very profitable. He started is own business doing just that in 1865 (he is considered by many to be the father of military surplus).

Bannerman bought up rifles, swords, bayonets, cannons, ammunition, black powder, and even canned goods to resell. This new family business grew quickly. Bannerman traveled extensively to make his military purchases. In 1872, he met his future wife, Helen Boyce, on a buying trip. They would go on to have three sons.

The Bannerman Business Grows More Successful and He Buys an Island

As the business continued to grow, it moved several times throughout the New York City area. The "neighbors" of Bannerman's office buildings and the city itself, became a little nervous about the large stores of munitions, cartridges, explosives, and other items. This would come to head when Bannerman traveled to Havana, Cuba in 1898. He successfully purchased almost all of the captured Spanish Arms, ammunition, explosives, and other items from the Spanish American War. Warehouses were overflowing, and the increasingly anxious city and region changed their laws. The Bannerman Business was forced to find a place store the bulk of their military surplus outside the city limits.

While canoeing along the Hudson, Bannerman's son David discovered Pollepel Island and brought it to his dad's attention. Deeming it a safe and isolated area to keep his surplus, Bannerman purchased the island from the Taft family in 1900. Bannerman had big plans for the island.

He knew this island was in full view of the commuter trains, and numerous merchant ships that passed in large numbers on the Hudson River. He decided he wanted to not just construct an area to store his goods, but something that would draw attention and be more eye-catching than advertising on a billboard. He began to piece ideas together from all over Europe and his travels, but he was influenced by his native Scotland and its impressive fortresses. He drew ideas on hotel stationary and other scraps of paper. He wouldn't just build a storage facility, he'd build an ornate castle!

Bannerman's Castle and the Island Arsenal

Construction on Bannerman's Scottish influenced castle began in 1901.

NEW YORK
Bannerman Castle

However, he didn't just begin construction on his ammunition storage warehouse, he and his wife had a smaller "castle" constructed. This would be the family summer house on the island and it featured beautiful gardens and terraces. The ever resourceful Bannerman would incorporate bayonets to reinforce concrete, and other decorative elements from his stores and surplus in all the buildings.

Francis Bannerman with artificial harbor
Public Domain

Bannerman also had an artificial harbor created (a breakaway) around the island with towers. The munitions and surplus would travel through the harbor to the island to be stored until sold.

The constriction of Bannerman's Castle dragged on in stages. As it did, ever the smart marketer, he made sure that one of the items visible early on and impossible to miss on the castle, from the sight of commuter trains and boats, was the large "Bannerman's Island Arsenal" along its castle walls. His idea worked and it became a focal point of Hudson River travelers. It also helped catapult the success of the military surplus business.

Bannerman created a catalogue to showcase the surplus he had for sale. In another smart move, he marketed to potential customers in pulp magazines, cowboy and wild west periodicals, and more. So he began to see business not just from governments and military surplus fans, but many others. Because of this catalogue and other efforts he started to sell to entertainments acts like **Buffalo Bill's Wild West Show**, rodeos, vaudeville acts, movie producers, circuses, and more. His inventory went beyond mere weaponry and uniforms, as he reportedly had a table owned by George Washington, and arctic equipment from Admiral Perry's trip to the North Pole. He was even reportedly the source for 50 percent of the commemorative cannons placed in public places.

Surprisingly, with all the war materials he profited from, Bannerman considered himself to be a man of peace. He was a member of the St. Andrews Society, and founded Caledonian Hospital. He was active in boy's club organizations, taking them to the island during the summer months. Bannerman hoped that humanity would learn to settle their differences through other means, and that his stores would become a "Museum to Lost Arts".

Bannerman was also considered very generous. Long before the U.S. would enter the first World War, he was outfitting British regiments at his own expense. In fact, by 1918 he was donating large amounts of military equipment to the allies fighting World War I. Unfortunately, Bannerman did-

NEW YORK
Historic Haunts of the North II

n't live to see his castle fully realized, he died that same year (1918) in November and construction stopped on his castle.

The Castle, Island, and Business after Bannerman's Death

Francis Bannerman's family continued to run his business after his death. In August 1920, 200 tons of shell and powder that Bannerman had stored on the island in one of the Castle's powder houses exploded destroying a large portion of the building. This explosion reportedly broke windows for miles in all directions. It also blew a chunk of the Castle Wall hundreds of feet

Bannerman Castle with collapsed wall
Public Domain

across the Hudson River, to land on the train tracks. This would tie up the train for hours. Bannerman's wife, nearby (just getting up from her hammock), narrowly avoided being hit by a piece of debris, but still had her eardrums ruptured by the shockwave. This explosion was attributed by the more superstitious to dark spirits on the island, but officials claimed after investigating, that lightning had struck one of the flagpoles, igniting two tons of explosives. The misfortune would continue.

In 1950 a cargo ship that was caught in a huge storm on the Hudson, crashed into the island and exploded, creating even more damage. Not long after the cargo ship incident, the local ferry that connected "Bannerman Island" to the mainland, sank. With the island hard to reach, the family tried to sell much of their stores. The Smithsonian also got much of it.

In 1967, The Jackson Hole Preserve bought the island and donated it to the people of the state of New York for parkland. The island was opened in 1968 as a public space, including the offering of tours. Sadly, in 1969 the buildings caught fire (a suggested case of arson). The fire destroyed the remaining ceilings and floors of Bannerman's Castle building, and left only outer brick and concrete walls. What was left was determined to be too big of a hazard, and Pollepel Island was ruled off limits to the public.

Pollepel Island and Bannerman Castle Since

In 1993, the **Bannerman Castle Trust** was founded by a group of hoping to preserve the remaining structures, and its history, Among these individuals was Jane Bannerman, a Campbell descendant, and wife of Charles Bannerman, Francis Bannerman's grandson. The Trust worked with the State

NEW YORK
Bannerman Castle

of New York to preserve and promote the Castle and Island and reopen them to the public. They started with kayak and hard-hat tours. Under their direction, a dock and stairway that leads to the Castle ruins was constructed with the help of nearby West Point Cadets. Volunteers have also created amazing gardens near Bannerman Castle in the spirit of Francis Bannerman's wife Helen.

Unfortunately, in 2009 a big section of the outer walls of Bannerman Castle collapsed. This necessitated the use of large metal braces to shore up the remaining building. Since then there have reportedly been signs of further decay and collapse.

Bannerman Castle with wall braces and trails visible
Courtesy Maryamh 111
Wikimedia Creative Commons

The Trusts mission to preserve the site as a historical, educational, and cultural location has never been more important. They've cleared and cleaned the island, making trails and buildings more accessible, and restored the Bannerman's summer house as a sort of mini-museum. They've also held unusual events to draw attention and raise monies, including notably, a performance of Dracula (and other plays), and recreated a meal from the Titanic. They've also added tours, where the guides sometimes mention that Bannerman Castle and the Island is haunted!

The Ghosts of Pollepel Island and Bannerman Castle

"The sloop continued labouring and rocking, as if she would have rolled her mast overboard. She seemed in continual danger either of upsetting or of running on shore. In this way she drove quite through the highlands, until she had passed Pollopol's Island, where, it is said, the jurisdiction of the Dunderberg potentate ceases."
—excerpt from the "The Storm-Ship," by Washington Irving

Long before Francis Bannerman, there were stories of a tribe of Goblins that controlled the winds and the water and used them to cause

Goblin from Children's Fairytale 19th Century Public Domain

93

NEW YORK
Historic Haunts of the North II

the sinking of boats in the Hudson River. Washington Irving heard these stories of the tribe of goblins that inhabited the island. He also learned that many people feared the island and believed it to be cursed. n his short story "The Storm-Ship", he detailed that Pellopol Island marked the northern end of the domain of the Heer of Dunderburg, a Dutch Goblin King, This Goblin King proved fatal to many sailing ships passing through the Hudson Highlands. Dutch sailors claimed for centuries to encounter those goblins and paid tribute when they sailed through the region.

There are numerous reports of paranormal activity connected to the ships that may have suffered the Goblin King's wrath. In one instance, a ship reportedly sank near the island centuries ago in the frozen water. Many believe the crew haunts the river, river banks, and the Island. There have been reports of a ghost ship being sailed by a ghostly crew. During big storms you can supposedly sometimes hear the disembodied cries from the crew calling for help.

Some of these unfortunate crewman have reportedly returned as "ghost imps." These ghost imps are said to predate the American Revolution, and have reportedly haunted the the region from Haverstraw Bay (the widest portion of the Hudson River), to Pollopel Island. These imps supposedly manifest and try to warn ships of the hazardous waters and dangerous items just below. To this day sailors tip their hats to thank them for their protection on the Hudson and near Pollopel Island.

Other Paranormal Activity on Pollopel Island

For decades visitors to the Island have encountered apparitions and other paranormal activity. Some have suggested this might be because Francis Bannerman included a foundation stone from the house of the massacred MacDonalds in Glencoe Scotland (1692) in his castle. That would certainly be an item with possible paranormal attachments. One of these restless souls is reportedly the MacDonald's descendant, Francis Bannerman himself.

Bannerman's ghost has been spotted and is reported to be active on Pollopel Island. Tour guides believe he makes himself known most often by turning over and dislodging bricks and stones at the Castle. These pieces of the former Castle seemingly activate of their own accord, with no wind or cascades from the crumbling structure to explain their sudden motion.

Another spirit reportedly encountered on the Island is the very person the place have been named for, Polly Pell. She has been seen walking the island looking out at the river. Many believe her spirit is still on the island because it was an important place in her life.

Final Thoughts on Pollopel Island and Bannerman Castle

The Hudson Valley has long been thought to be haunted, and reportedly

NEW YORK
Bannerman Castle

possesses a magical quality, goblins or not. For this reason, and the stories around it, it caught the attention of one of my favorite authors, Washington Irving. In fact, he collected many local legends for material for many of his stories including "The Storm-Ship" and its ill-fated ghost ship on the Hudson near Pollopel Island. Irving's home at Sunnyside can be seen from the same trains where passengers can view the island and Bannerman Castle.

Bannerman Castle itself is an amazing structure which has become famous in pictures, in big newspapers, and even used in films. However, without help it may not be with us long. I encourage my readers to visit, volunteer, sponsor, or donate to The Bannerman Castle Trust. You can also go to their website or find their pages on social media sites. Let's help preserve this scenic Historic Haunt.

The Bannerman Castle Trust
P.O. Box 843
Glenham, NY 12527-0843

www.bannermancastle.org

Bannerman Castle with boat ramp photograph courtesy Friedo Wikimedia Creative Commons

NEW YORK
Historic Haunts of the North II

THE GHOSTS OF BASEBALL'S PAST AND PRESENT

National Baseball Hall of Fame and Museum, Cooperstown, New York

National Baseball Hall of Fame and Museum, courtesy Kenneth C. Zirkel Wikipedia Creative Commons

"Baseball is a game dominated by vital ghosts; it's a fraternity, like no other we have, of the active and the no-longer-so, the living and the dead."
—Richard Gilman, American Drama and Literary critic

"The one constant through all the years, Ray, has been baseball. America has rolled by like an army of steamrollers. It has been erased like a blackboard, rebuilt and erased again. But baseball has marked the time. This field, this game: it's a part of our past, Ray. It reminds us of all that once was good and could be again. Oh... people will come Ray. People will most definitely come. "
— Spoken by "Terence Mann" (James Earl Jones), from **Field of Dreams**, THE baseball and ghost movie, and one of the best baseball movies ever!

Baseball is one of our country's favorite sports. Like the seams on the ball, it seems to be able to stitch together a variety of fans from a variety of backgrounds. Sometimes these fans have very little in common, but their love of the game. Baseball holds a high place in the National identity, with hot dogs, and apple pie, an essential thread of Americana. In Cooperstown, New York you can find a famous, three-story brick building, with a wide ranging array

NEW YORK
National Baseball Hall of Fame and Museum

of exhibits and displays, as well as theaters, and a library, all dedicated to celebrating our National Pastime. For those fans, who feel they're already familiar with the National Baseball Hall of Fame and Museum, I may be about to throw your a curve ball. For others who've had experiences, this won't seem like it's coming out of left field. Many fans of the game, and its history, feel the Hall of Fame is haunted! However, we'll touch base on that in a bit, let's take a closer look at the Hall itself and its history.

The Creation of Cooperstown's Famous Hall of Fame

Sam Crane. a popular sportswriter, was reportedly the first person to suggest making a memorial to the great sport in Cooperstown. Crane, came from a position of knowledge of the game, he had managed and played baseball for a decade in the 19th century. At the time, Cooperstown was thought to be the place where the game originated. It was reported to be a variation of "Town Ball" and thus a creation of American Abner Doubleday, who supposedly organized a group to play, and not the British game of "Rounders", that many people attributed it to.

Abner Doubleday public domain

Doubleday was a career United States Army Officer, a theosophist (thus a believer in spirits), and a Civil War hero. He reportedly fired the first shot in defense of Fort Sumter at the beginning of the Civil War, and later fought at the Battle of Gettysburg. Doubleday was reported to have invented baseball in Cooperstown itself in 1839 and proof was offered along with a diagram that Doubleday supposedly made, showing the changes to the field and position of players. Based on this and other evidence, the (highly biased) Mills Commission, officially declared him the inventor in 1908, 15 years after his death (Doubleday, for his part, never claimed to have invented it). Since then, we've learned Doubleday was actually at West Point in 1839, and Alexander Cartwright is the true "Father of Baseball", having developed the game (based on Rounders) in the 1840's. The controversy continued for some time. A middle ground was reached when Cartwright was added to the Hall and events were added in his honor. Thankfully, this controversy didn't hurt the spirit and love of baseball. In fact, the false notion that it was developed here by Doubleday, was instrumental in the early marketing to help create and promote the Hall of Fame.

Besides Abner Doubleday, and sports writer Sam Crane, there were others hoping to see a Hall of Fame happen. A gentleman named Stephen Carlton Clark was one of the early proponents for a Hall of Fame in Cooperstown. Clark was the heir of the Singer Sewing Fortune, and a big baseball fan. Clark was hoping to bring tourists to the Village. He hoped to ease the prob-

NEW YORK
Historic Haunts of the North II

lems for the local economy created by the Great Depression and Prohibition. Clark had the building to house the Hall constructed. The opening coincided with the celebrated "Centennial of Baseball", marking its first hundred years.

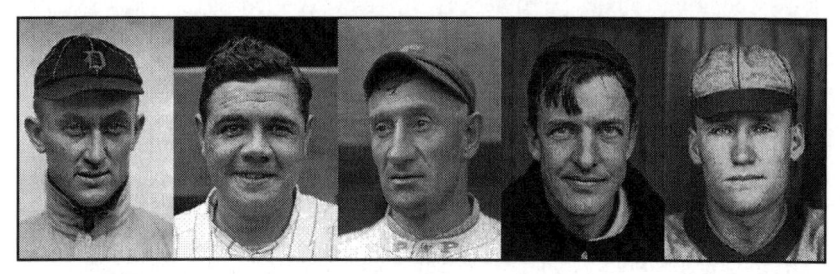

1936 Hall of Fame Class: Ty Cobb, Babe Ruth, Honus Wagner, Christy Mathewson, Walter Johnson - Public Domain image

The inaugural Hall of Fame class inducted in 1936 was: Ty Cobb, Walter Johnson, Christy Mathewson, Babe Ruth, and Honus Wagner. As of this writing, some 346 people have been inducted into the Hall of Fame. Other parts of the building, including the museum, opened three years later in 1942.

The museum consists of many rooms full of amazing baseball memorabilia from some of the greatest moments and players of all time. However, it's not just the players that are enshrined here. The Hall of Fame also holds the managers, umpires, executives, and pioneers of baseball, that have helped elevate this amazing sport. There's even nods given to writers, broadcasters, and celebrities who have helped baseball find its sweet spot with the American public. All are represented in this amazing structure.

On the building's first floor you'll find a theater that plays the iconic routine "Who's on First", by the legendary comedy duo of Abbott and Costello. This floor also contains some of the building's most popular attractions. Among them, the "Inductee Room", where the first players inducted into the Hall through 1939 are shown, and the "Plaque Gallery", the most recognized area of the Museum. The Plaque Gallery contains a room with over 300 bronze plaques of all the members inducted into the Hall of Fame, including one of my favorites, Billy Williams (class of 1987). I got to meet him personally in 1996 (in case you didn't know, I am a HUGE **Chicago Cubs** fan). The first floor also contains the "Perez-Steele Art Gallery" which presents art and

Plaque Gallery courtesy WKnight 94 Wikimedia Creative Commons

NEW YORK
National Baseball Hall of Fame and Museum

other media related to baseball. All of these are a warmup for the building's second floor.

*Second Floor courtesy Kenneth C. Zirkel
Wikimedia Creative Commons*

*Whole New Ballgame
courtesy Seanbarnett
Wikimedia Creative Commons*

The popular second floor contains another theater with replica stadium seats. This leads into an area called "the Game". This section of the building contains most of the artifacts all set up in a fashion to present a baseball timeline. It includes special recognition areas and mentions to certain players, eras, and groups. "A Whole New Ballgame" follows "the Game". This exhibit finishes the timeline taking us through the last 45 years of the sport, to get us to the game we know today. What the Hall of Fame does not seem to mention, and what some balk at, is the fact that the place might have a haunted side. It turns out, there may be some famous souls at the Hall taking a spectral seventh inning stretch throughout the building.

The Haunted Hall of Fame?

Baseball is no stranger to eerie occurrences or superstition, ask any player in a slump or on a streak. For generations there have been stories of the supernatural connected to the sport, like baseball great Roberto Clemente dreaming of his own death, and curses like the "Curse of the Billy Goat" (connected to my own beloved Chicago Cubs). In many cases, paranormal incidents seem to be connected to personal items "empowered" or linked through traumatic or momentous events. There are over 200 members of the Hall of Fame who are deceased, and their personal items, like baseball bats, gloves, uniforms,

NEW YORK
Historic Haunts of the North II

helmets, and other items, are among the artifacts on display. With all this wonderful baseball memorabilia and personal items, it is no surprise that there could be attachments and the museum could be haunted. If any of these dead players (with possible paranormal connections) wanted to take a swing at manifesting, and getting back in the game, there are plenty of souls in the bullpen, on the bench, or represented in the Hall that could be on deck!

I'll try to cover all the bases when it comes to paranormal activity at the Hall of Fame. We'll start with the more common and more general reports throughout the building. These reports include ethereal voices and sounds, spectral figures, strange light anomalies, and disembodied footsteps, even the sound of baseball cleats. Shadow figures have also been seen in different areas, especially around personal items that are on display.

Among these paranormally active personal items are Joe DiMaggio's Yankee's Locker, Hank Aaron's uniform, and Barry Bond's asterix ball (the homer he hit that broke Aaron's record). Overnight security guards have echoed these claims, and mentioned encountering men's restroom doors near these items, that open and close on their own. These same guards have also described the elevators near these (and similar items), that travel randomly to certain floors or just up and down, with no one else in the building and no one to activate the buttons. The elevators have bee checked for mechanical issues several times. According to staff members and guests, this is nothing compared to parts of the Inductee area.

Hank Aaron's Braves uniform Public Domain

The second section of the Hall of Fame that we'll cover that is known to be very paranormally active, is the Plaque Room. This is where most of t he inductees are represented. There have been accounts here of unexplained noises, unnerving sensations (akin to being watched), and male voices speaking or shouting. Witnesses seem to assign most of these phantom voices to two specific former players.

Ty Cobb and "Shoeless" Joe Jackson

"Ty Cobb wanted to play, but none of us could stand the (S.O.B.) when we were alive, so we told him to stick it! "
—paraphrased quote from the ghost of "Shoeless" Joe Jackson (Ray Liotta), also from **Field of Dreams**

Ty Cobb Hall of Fame Plaque Courtesy RasputinAXP Creative Commons

Some paranormal researchers ascribe to the idea that people with stronger personalities are more likely to

100

NEW YORK

National Baseball Hall of Fame and Museum

come back as ghosts or spirits. If that's true, than Ty Cobb certainly fits the bill. Many guests and staff at the Hall of Fame describe hearing everything from whispers to loud voices from the area of Ty Cobb's plaque. Not all of these disembodied conversations are pleasant (reportedly like the man himself). However, the most common disembodied voice heard in the Plaque Room has been suggested to belong to "Shoeless" Joe Jackson.

The Restless Spirit of "Shoeless" Joe

"Shoeless" Joe Jackson was one of the greatest players baseball has ever known (and a central spirit to the storyline of the baseball movie classic ***Field of Dreams***). Unfortunately, he was associated with the infamous "Black Sox Scandal", in which the 1919 Chicago White Sox players were involved in a conspiracy to fix the World Series. Jackson proclaimed his innocence until his death (a fact his teammates also testified to). During that World Series he led both teams in several categories and set World Series records with 12 base hits (pretty odd behavior for someone who supposedly threw the game). He is one of the most fiercely debated figures in all of sports. The Baseball Hall of Fame maintains a list of players that are "permanently ineligible". There are others on the list (like Pete Rose), but Jackson is the most high profile and most qualified. Perhaps that's why his spirit has been thought to speak out.

"Shoeless" Joe Jackson
Public Domain

Jackson's spirit is thought to be haunting the Plaque Room. His disembodied voice is said to be pleading for his inclusion among the inductees in the Hall, Jackson apparently wants his own plaque. He is most often encountered during the summer months when the Hall of Fame stays open later.

Teddy Ballgame

The third distinct ghost said to make itself known, in the Hall is that of Ted Williams, nicknamed "Teddy Ballgame." His spirit seems to be encountered most often near the exhibit dedicated to him. Shadow figures have been seen in the Hall of Fame connected to or near this exhibit. In life, Williams was known to be great at, and made a habit of, giving advice and pep talks to kids. He seems to be keeping up his habit in his afterlife as well. Several younger baseball fans have been "treated" to motivational speeches or advice when near his exhibit. This despite the fact that there is no voice component to his display at the Hall of Fame.

Ted Williams
Baseball Card
Public Domain

101

NEW YORK
Historic Haunts of the North II

The Spectral Spectators

Certain probing groups have had a front row seat to activity at the Hall of Fame. Several paranormal investigative groups have gone to the Hall of Fame hoping to capture evidence. Many have learned that the undead aren't always willing to play ball. Some have had more success. Televised ghost hunting groups have recorded EVPs (especially in the Plaque Room). They've also personally experienced the activity involving the men's restroom doors that the security staff claimed. Other groups have detailed reports of an apparition in uniform, seen on the baseball field, and the connected "crack" of a bat hitting a ball. As a baseball fan, this is a pretty unmistakable sound. Lastly, paranormal seekers described phantom figures in the "Pride and Passion" exhibit, which details the history of African Americans in baseball.

Final Thoughts from a Baseball Fan

I'm not the first writer or entertainer to feel connected to darker stories and also be intrigued by baseball. **Dracula's** Bela Lugosi was friends with Babe Ruth, and Vincent Price (one of my favorites) was a diehard Dodgers fan. Even The **Twilight Zone's** Rod Serling created episodes connected to baseball and was himself a devoted fan.

To diehards like me, the National Baseball Hall of Fame and Museum in Cooperstown serves as the central point of baseball in the U.S. The Hall and the city, are permanently connected. So much so, that Cooperstown has become synonymous for the site, and shorthand to baseball fans for induction into the Hall of Fame. This amazing place has over 40,000 artifacts, 3 million library items, 140,000 baseball cards, learning centers, programs, and other features, that make this a home run for any baseball fans.

Vincent Price at Dodgers Game Author's Collection

I haven't personally made it there yet, but you better believe this is a future must stop for me! Ever since I was a little girl I dreamed of visiting here (and that was before I ever knew it was haunted). I look forward to walking the halls and hope to meet one of the ghostly greats of baseball's past. This is a Historic Haunt that's definitely in my wheelhouse. And oh yeah…
GO CUBS GO

LEGEND OF THE LINCOLN GHOST TRAIN HUDSON VALLEY, NEW YORK

New York and Other Areas

" I now leave, not knowing when, or whether ever, I may return."
— Spoken by President- Elect Abraham Lincoln from the back of a railway car in Springfield, Illinois in 1861

"Now he belongs to the ages."
—reportedly spoken by Secretary of War, Edwin Stanton moments after Lincoln took his final breath

Lincoln Funeral Train
Public Domain

The 16th President of the United States of America, Abraham Lincoln, was assassinated on April 15th, 1865 at Ford's Theatre in Washington D.C. by John Wilkes Booth. Most of us remember this from our history books. Less well known are the details of what happened to Lincoln's body after the President had passed. Many know there was a funeral train, but few know much more than that. Especially surprising is the fact that Lincoln's Funeral Train seems to come back at times as a spectral locomotive!

Prefacing This Entry and Correcting Myself

I covered the passing of President Lincoln by assassination in ***Historic Haunts of the North*** (see the section on "Ford's Theatre"). In that story, I also briefly mentioned Lincoln's Funeral Train and it's 11 official stops. After sending the first North book to print and working on this second one, conflicting research materials suggested to me that the train might have actually made 13 official stops. However, before we look at some of these stops, let's take a little closer look at the moments before the train's departure and what happened later during it's historical trek across parts of the United States.

After Lincoln's Passing

Mary Todd Lincoln, First Lady, and Lincoln's widow, wanted to get her husband's body quickly and quietly to the cemetery to bury him. She would be talked out of these wishes by then **Secretary of War**, Edwin Stanton. Stanton felt there was a collective need for Americans to mourn their beloved

103

NEW YORK
Historic Haunts of the North II

President face-to-face. Lincoln's body would be heading for his burial site as planned, however, Mary Todd Lincoln gave her consent to a rather unusual request by Stanton. The President's coffin would be transported in such a way as to allow it to retrace the path of the Whistle Stops Lincoln made earlier on his way to the capitol (during his inauguration). Stanton also convinced Lincoln's widow to allow stops in several cities along the route. During these stops, the upper half of the casket would be lifted for public viewing, a final bit of closure for a grieving nation.

Lincoln would be transported in a special railway car originally intended with him in mind, but not for this sad purpose. The Federal Government had created the first private car for Presidential use. It was meant to take him around the country in an effort to reunite a divided nation after the Civil War. Lincoln never stepped inside the car while alive. Thus the car became "The Funeral Car United States". The train that carried it would be dubbed "The Lincoln Special". Lincoln's portrait would be fastened to the locomotive's front. The train would have 9 cars in total, and substitute locomotives at the front at various points.

The choice of trains for transporting Lincoln's body was appropriate since he had built a successful legal practice and career as a protector and promoter of railway law. Lincoln saw the potential in this transportation. He pushed for the Transcontinental Railroad to unite the nation "from sea to shining sea".

Leading Into the Journey

Lincoln's black mahogany coffin had spent two nights lying in state. It was transported by hearse on April 21, 1865 to the train depot. His coffin was carried by soldiers and accompanied by an honor guard. It was also accompanied by many members of Lincoln's cabinet, including Ulysses S. Grant and Edwin Stanton. Lincoln's body in his coffin was placed in the funeral car along with the body of his son Willie (who had died sometime before). Mary Todd Lincoln would not travel with the train, being too distraught to do so. However, several members of her family, including cousins, Lincoln's brothers-in-law, and his eldest son Robert did.

Robert Todd Lincoln

Lincoln's eldest son Robert had graduated Harvard in 1864. He had also attended its Law School for a time. After graduating, he was commissioned a captain and placed on the staff of Ulysses S. Grant (reportedly a favor from Grant for his mother, who was trying to keep him out the worst of the war and thus out of harm's way).

Robert Lincoln
Public Domain

Robert Todd Lincoln was present for Robert E. Lee's surrender at Appomattox Court House. Ironically, according to historical records, he had a near fatal accident in Jersey City, New Jersey in late 1864 or early 1865. The most well known actor in America, the famous Edwin Booth saved his life from a train ledge. Booth was a staunch supporter of the Union, and unfortunately for him, the brother of John Wilkes Booth, the man who later murdered Robert's father.

The Lincoln Special's Passengers and Departure

Besides Robert, an honor guard and soldiers were present on the train, as well as Lincoln's beloved friend, and longtime (self-appointed) bodyguard Ward Hill Lamon. Lamon was in Richmond, Virginia on an errand for Lincoln at the time of the assassination.

The train also held an embalmer tasked with preserving the President's body on the trip. There were some 150 passengers on the trip at departure (it would swell to 300 by the end of the nearly 1,700 mile journey). The train left the Baltimore & Ohio (B&O) Railroad Station after much subdued fanfare for its sombre trip. Edwin Stanton may have suspected a large outpouring of affection for the deceased President, but he could scarcely imagine what would follow. Still, Stanton and others had some trepidation about the train's first official stop in Baltimore.

Heading to Baltimore

The train progressed towards its stop in Baltimore. As it traveled it never exceeded 20 mph. In fact, it traveled a large part of its journey at a speed closer to 5 mph. Ideally this would allow people to see it and Lincoln's railcar in particular. The passengers on the train started to take note of the behavior of the people they encountered outside the vehicle. All along the route, men took off their hats for mile upon mile as the train passed. Women whispered prayers, and hymns were sung by choruses. The nation's newspapers published listings of the train's stops and schedule for the public to read. This included publications in the city of Baltimore.

The reaction the public would have to the train in Baltimore was unknown. Baltimore was John Wilkes Booth's hometown and it was also known to have some inhabitants with much enmity towards Lincoln. Only a few years earlier, Lincoln had traveled through the city incognito due to the hostility felt toward him and reported assassination plots.

This would not be the reaction on this sad occasion. Over 30,000 spectators attended the procession and the train stop. Remarkably, for Lincoln's Funeral Train, black and white mourners came out in massive numbers, side by side in the rain, to pay homage to the President.

This type of reaction would only escalate during the trip. The train's arrival would also be marked by a surge of civic pride that seemed to require each stop along the route to prepare more and more extravagant hearses, memorial

NEW YORK
Historic Haunts of the North II

areas, and displays for the President's coffin.

People traveled for miles to camp along the railway tracks, hoping to catch a glimpse of Lincoln's coffin through the railcar window. Bonfires lit the countryside for miles along the train's tracks, illuminating its path through the dead of night. Crowds in every town gathered to see the procession. American's came out in droves, even in bad weather or in the wee hours to pay tribute to the Great Emancipator. They communed in city after city. Preacher Henry Ward Beecher declared, *"The nation rises up at every stage of his coming. Cities and states are his pallbearers."*

Philadelphia's Brotherly Love

In Philadelphia, tens of thousands of Americans mourned as they escorted the President's coffin to Independence Hall. Lincoln's coffin was placed at the foot of the Liberty Bell. Approximately 150,000 people passed it to honor Lincoln. The crowds would continue to grow.

*Lincoln procession
Public Domain*

New York

At the time of "The Lincoln Special's" arrival, New York was the most populous state in the Union. The train would make official stops in New York City, Albany, and Buffalo. Over a half million spectators came out in Manhattan alone! This is also the city where a 6 year old Theodore Roosevelt could see the coffin and procession from his second-floor window. It was estimated that some 125,000 people filed past the coffin as it lay on display in City Hall.

*Lincoln procession New York
Public Domain*

All through the state New Yorkers showed up in large numbers. In Buffalo, like Teddy Roosevelt, future President Grover Cleveland would see Lincoln's body. Unfortunately, by the time the train left New York, the President's corpse was definitely starting to show signs of decay. The embalmer had to add more chalk like makeup and take steps to cover aspects. The newspapers of the time commented on this,

*Lincoln procession Buffalo, NY
Public Domain*

NEW YORK
Lincoln's Ghost Train

remarking that the former President's face and his appearance was a "ghostly shadow" of its former self.

The Train Moves Towards its Last Stop

As Lincoln's funeral train made it way westward towards the Midwest, the region (which had long claimed Lincoln) became even more intense in their show of feelings towards their fallen President. In Chicago a public viewing was held in which the line of mourners stretched more than a mile. The train reached the end of the line on May 3rd, with its arrival in Springfield, Illinois, the state capitol. A 24 hour viewing was held there. Lincoln's coffin was closed on May 4th. An official funeral service was held as Lincoln's body, and that of his son, were placed in a limestone vault and the doors and iron gates were shut. Lincoln's body was interred at Oak Ridge Cemetery. Over the years his body has been moved 17 times, including almost being stolen and held for ransom.

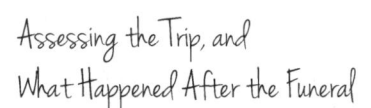

Lincoln procession Chicago
Public Domain

Lincoln burial site
Springfield
Courtesy Robert Lawton
Wikimedia Creative
Commons

Assessing the Trip, and What Happened After the Funeral

It became very apparent that the Lincoln Funeral Train provided more than an opportunity for grief-stricken Americans to say goodbye. It became a huge emotional release for a nation that had bottled up its collective grief for the last 4 years. The funeral train passed through 400 cities and towns in 7 states. It was the first National Commemoration of a President's death by rail.

It was estimated that over 1 million Americans viewed Lincoln's corpse directly (some waiting in lines over 5 hours long). Millions more saw the President's coffin along the route. As much as 25% of the U.S. population at the time (about 8 million people), may have had some contact with the train and a view of Lincoln's coffin.

The Junior Lincoln After the Train Ride

After the Funeral, Robert Todd Lincoln would go on to serve as Secretary of War under President James A. Garfield and Chester A. Arthur. He would also serve as minister to Great Britain in the Benjamin Harrison administra-

107

NEW YORK
Historic Haunts of the North II

tion. Many tried to persuade him to run for the Presidency himself. However, he was nearby for three different Presidential assassinations. He was at the nearby White House when his father was killed (having turned down an invite to attend the theatre with his parents that evening). He was an eyewitness when President James A. Garfield was shot. He was also just outside the area when President William McKinley was shot. He was well aware of this strange coincidence (perhaps that's why he never ran for higher office). He stated, "there is a certain fatality about presidential functions when I am present." He would go on to become a highly successful lawyer, and later, President of the Pullman Train Company, after its founder died in 1897.

Lincoln's original Funeral Car was destroyed by fire in 1911on a Minneapolis, Minnesota sidetrack. A recreated version of the Lincoln Funeral Car can be found at the amazing **Lincoln Train Museum** in Gettysburg, Pennsylvania (within walking distance of the site of the former President's famous address). However, paranormal fans might be intrigued to learn that many have seen the spectral form of this locomotive along the historic route.

Lincoln's Ghost Train

Many in the paranormal field feel that traumatic events and large outpourings of emotional energies tend to mark and can "fuel" ghostly activity in an area. The amount of emotion pouring out from million of grief-stricken Americans could easily be considered enough to fit the bill. Many have claimed to see the phantom train in various locations along the old route for years. In fact, there are frequent unnerving encounters with the ghost train described by railroad employees over the years. It is identified as such by witnesses who claim to see Lincoln's image on the front of the train or with his coffin on the back.

The spectral appearance of the locomotive and cars is often marked with a surge of unusual phenomenon. According to witnesses, a cold rush of air along the tracks suddenly springs up (without current weather to explain it). Viewers describe a chilling feel to the air just before the ghost train's arrival and the apparition is sometimes accompanied by sounds of a ghostly whistle and spectral smoke.

The manifestations of the train seem to take one of three forms. The first is as a ghostly blur. The second, more common encounter involves a slow-moving spectral train traveling along the same rails. Sometimes this train is empty, sometimes the President's coffin can be seen. The third, and most disturbing collection of reports, involves the train passing with skeletal passengers and a group of blue coated skeletons surrounding Lincoln's flag-draped coffin. When the ghost train has passed, clocks have been reported to be six minutes late (perhaps the amount of time it took the original slow-moving train to pass). In all of these ethereal manifestations the passing of a real train nearby will cause the ghost train to disappear into thin air.

The train is spotted most often in April, often on full moon nights. It has been encountered all along the historic train's path. but more often and more strongly in New York (perhaps due to the energy released by its large mourning crowds). There are reports of it at **Grand Central Station**, which didn't exist at the time of the historical trip, but the halls there did. For many years, there were reports of the train appearing in Albany on April 25th/26th, the anniversary of its arrival and departure. It was said to appear at midnight. Sounds of the train and funeral music are frequently heard before it vanishes.

Final Thoughts on the Ghost Train

There are no shortage of tales and campfire stories of spectral locomotives. Among these, the tale of this one, Lincoln's ticket to the afterlife, is unique, and remains the best in my opinion. The train doesn't seem to appear as frequently as before, but is still talked about and is an awesome story connected to one of my favorite presidents. I'd like to think it doesn't appear as frequently anymore because President Lincoln is now at peace. Regardless, Lincoln's Ghost Train is one of the first I've encountered that seems to traverse multiple states. Considering Lincoln's place in the country's history, this train remains a true Historic Haunt!

NEW YORK
Historic Haunts of the North II

SPIES AND SAD SPIRITS AT RAYNHAM HALL

Raynham Hall, Oyster Bay New York

The American Revolution is one of the most fascinating times in recorded history (at least in this humble author's opinion). Most students of history are familiar with America's Founding Fathers and the major landmark events that helped forge this country's origins. However, many are unfamiliar with the smaller events and historical figures whose contributions were equally as essential.

Raynham Hall courtesy Idosyterbay Wikimedia Creative Commons

Among these George Washington's Culpepper Spy Ring. In part, located at the Townsend homestead in Oyster Bay in New York.

The Coming of the Homestead

Samuel Townsend purchased a piece of property in 1738 which consisted of a four room frame house and featured an orchard across the street and a meadow leading to the harbor. By 1740 he enlarged the home to eight rooms and dubbed it "The Homestead". The Townsend family was one of the founding families of Oyster Bay.

Samuel and his wife Sarah Stoddard Townsend had eight children and had a thriving mercantile business owning four ships. Townsend brought in molasses, pottery, lumber, wine, fabric, die, and rum. The Townsends also operated a general store from their home offering; spices, sugar, smoked ham, nails, ink stands, and more. Townsend was also a Justice of the Peace and a member of the New York Provincial Congress which voted to ratify the Declaration of Independence.

Despite Townsend's support of the Patriot's cause, the town of Oyster Bay was equally divided with half claiming loyalty to the crown and half to the Patriot cause. Following the Patriot's defeat at the Battle of Long Island (in autumn of 1776), the Townsend homestead came under British occupation by virtue of the Quartering Acts of 1765. The Townsend's were not happy, but were required by law to oblige.

NEW YORK

Spies and Sad Spirits at Raynham Hall

For a six-month period between 1778 and 1779 the home served as British headquarters for the Queen's Loyalist Rangers. This group was led by Lieut. Col. John Graves Simcoe. During this time, The Townsend home was also visited often by British Officer Maj. John Andre.

By all accounts, despite the occupation, the family and the troops got along well; especially Major John Andre, a likable fellow who befriended the whole family and Lieutenant Colonel Simcoe, who became enamored of Townsend's daughter, Sally. Ironically, the Townsends were not just patriots, but spies. Townsend's son Robert, had harnessed his British contacts from business and mercantile to spy for General George Washington, even becoming known as "Culpepper, Jr.", the second highest member of the spy ring itself. The occupying British forces were unaware of this. And despite this fact, Sally became enamored of Simcoe as well.

The Valentine and Sally's Choice

The Homestead was the site for the first known "American" Valentine's from Lieut. Col. Simcoe to Sally (also known by Sarah). Sally kept the Valentine (until her death at the age of 82) and never married, but played a major part in the war. It is said that Sally became privy to a very damaging letter or discussion between Lieut. Col. Simcoe and Maj. John Andre.

Col. Simcoe Painting later in life
Public Domain

The exchange between Simcoe and Andre involved the attempt to bribe Benedict Arnold to turn over the Fort at West Point. Sally had to decide whether her sense of patriotism was more important than her fondness for the two men. She chose the former and passed the info to her father. He in turn, passed it on to his son Robert, and ultimately to Washington and the American forces. Andre was captured in civilian attire with the evidence and hanged. Simcoe, despite his supposed fondness for Sally (Sarah), left the states and married another. The Townsend homestead was sold to various members of the family after the Revolutionary War.

Townsend's grandson, Solomon Townsend II, purchased the home in 1851 and started making several changes. He enlarged the home, and renamed it Raynham Hall after the family estates in England. He raised seven children here with his wife Helen Dekay.

Raynham Hall would stay in the family for some time, but would eventually pass to the Daughters of the American Revolution. Understanding its historical value in our country's founding, they maintained it as a tea room and historic site. Eventually, unable to afford the upkeep, they offered it to the town of Oyster Bay. The town took ownership and began some restoration

NEW YORK
Historic Haunts of the North II

projects to make parts of the house more closely resemble the Revolutionary era. Today it serves as a museum and a place where visitors can learn more about the Townsend's and the Culpepper Spy Ring, including sample codes and translations. They can also learn what has been known for some time, that Raynham Hall is haunted.

Raynham Haunts

Interestingly enough, chronicled reports of paranormal activity here only date back to Julia Weeks Cole (a family descendent), who lived in the house from 1914 to 1933. She wrote articles for a local paper about the spirits that haunted the place. In one of her accounts, an overnight guest was startled awake from a deep sleep by the sounds of a ghostly horse and rider outside the bedroom window. Mrs. Cole thought the ghost could be the spirit of Major Andre. However, this particular rider's ghost has also been encountered at Raynham's Hall in England, believed to be a sign of impending death in the family. Another ghost of England's Raynham Hall, the Brown Lady has more recently been encountered. Miss Cole also detailed in other articles the ghost of Robert Townsend, whose apparition was seen at times descending the front stairs.

Since Miss Cole's time, and more frequently during renovations (which tend to stir up paranormal activity), there have been numerous reports of other paranormal phenomenon. Among those reports are incidents of unexplained noises, disembodied footsteps that follow staff members and tours, as well as the phantom scents of pipe tobacco, wood fires, apple pie baking (from the kitchen area) and roses. It is believed that many of these noises can be attributed to the ghosts of a young boy or a former Irish servant, both have been seen.

The spirit of Major Andre has also been encountered since Mrs. Cole's time. Sometimes on horse back, typically riding up to the area near Sally's window as his spirit seems to be in a pleasant mood later when encountered, many have speculated he returns to let his dear friend Sally know he has forgiven her. At times during his appearance, her ghost has also been seen in the window.

Sally's Ghost and Simcoe

Sally never married and reportedly never got over Lieutenant Colonel Simcoe. Her ghost has been encountered numerous times. Psychics and others who visit her room describe a feeling of great sadness that may be connected to her. Her appearances are often marked by cold spots, and temperature drops of as much as 15 degrees. However, not every paranormal report details Sally's spirit as being unhappy.

Many believe that the spirits who are still here are the separated lovers, Sally and Simcoe. There is a preserved windowpane in the Museum attributed by many to Simcoe, that would attest to his fondness for Sally. Scratched on the window is a message to "The adorable Miss Sally Townsend".

Sally's Apparition

Sally is seen often in the home and on the grounds while Simcoe's ghost has been spotted alone often times appearing with a stern look upon his face. According to some paranormal reports, it seems that they are finally able to reunite. Sometimes their spirits are encountered together. Both look peaceful and blissful when in each other's spectral company.

I prefer to think of Sally and her valentine Simcoe's story happily. A true love story that was ended by war, but reunited in death. This is one of Historic Haunts' favorite haunted love stories. Whether you're a fan of the paranormal or Culpepper's Spy Ring and the early days of American History, Raynham Hall is a great place to investigate for yourself. The very dedicaed docents and workers at the former homestead seem to agree and also have a fondness for it and the history it's connected to. If you're not careful you may fall in love with it as well.

Raynham Hall and friendly staff
Public Domain

NEW YORK
Historic Haunts of the North II

THE BRONZE LADY, WASHINGTON IRVING, AND THE HEADLESS HORSEMAN AT SLEEPY HOLLOW CEMETERY

Sleepy Hollow Cemetery, Tarrytown, NY

Most of us have heard the name "Sleepy Hollow". The details of Washington Irving's iconic tale, including the region and the names of Ichabod Crane and the Headless Horseman, are a part of the fabric of America. However, what many literary fans and horror story fans may not know is that Washington Irving is buried right here in this Tarrytown, New York cemetery (along with many other famous figures). The general public is probably also unaware that the place is haunted, and the Headless Horseman is reportedly one of the haunts!

Sleeping Hollow Cemetery entrance Courtesy of Midnightdrearya Wikimedia Creative Commons

Sleepy Hollow Cemetery

Sleepy Hollow Cemetery was incorporated in 1849 as Tarrytown Cemetery. It is a non-sectarian burial ground that consists of approximately 90 acres. It is contiguous with, but separate from, the Old Dutch Church churchyard, which was the setting for Washington Irving's story, "The Legend if Sleepy Hollow".

There is also a private Rockefeller cemetery that shares a boundary with Sleepy Hollow Cemetery. Rockefeller is interred along with many other captains of industry, such as cosmetics queen Elizabeth Arden, Philanthropist Andrew Carnegie, Chrysler Corporation founder Walter Chrysler, and real estate moguls Harry and Leona Helmsley (among others). They are joined in eternal rest by numerous politicians and their children (including some of Alexander Hamilton's), and a bevy of artists, journalists, and well known writers. The obvious standout being Washington Irving (1783-1859) who is interred here.

The Legend of Sleepy Hollow Author's Collection

NEW YORK
Sleepy Hollow Cemetery

Irving's Beloved Tale

Washington Irving's famous tale has had a deep and lasting effect on the literary world, the cemetery, the area, and Tarrytown as a whole. In fact, the original cemetery's name was changed as a posthumous behest to honor the famous writer. His short story is extremely popular throughout the year, and especially during the Halloween Season. It has spawned movies, picture books, envelopes, stamps, and many other collectibles (some for sale in Tarrytown). Every year local celebrity and famed storyteller, Jonathan Kruk, regales groups with his spirited retellings of "The Legend of Sleepy Hollow". He has performed his narratives in the cemetery, in town, and at Washington Irving's Sunnyside (see ***Historic Haunts of the North***). However, Irving's story, and that of his unearthly chief antagonist, apparently don't end there! They are both a part of the ghostly after-hours activities at this famous cemetery.

The Legend of Sleepy Hollow Collectible Envelope Author's Collection

Storyteller Jonathan Kruk

Scary Spirits of the Cemetery

One of the more infamous sources of paranormal activity at the boneyard is the "Bronze Lady". The Bronze Lady is a larger-than-life statue commissioned by the widow of Civil War General Samuel Thomas. This towering figure is called "grief", and was intended as a memorial figure to be placed in front of Thomas' tomb. Today she rests in front of his mausoleum where she reportedly keeps a watchful eye. It is said if you approach the Lady, you may hear the disembodied sounds of her spectral weeping. Tears have reportedly been seen flowing from here eyes. Many claim this might be merely collecting water from rain or dew and easily dismiss it. Harder to dispel are the reports that claim if you look in the keyhole of the General's mausoleum, or knock on the door, you"ll have haunted or very bad dreams.

Despite the tales of otherworldly activity connected to the Lady, many tempt fate by trying to

The Bronze Lady Sleepy Hollow Cemetery courtesy Alex Matsuo Author of **Women of the Paranormal**

115

NEW YORK
Historic Haunts of the North II

interact with her statue directly. Some come to regret it. It is said if you sit or rest in her lap, her watery tears become tears of blood. It is also thought that if you strike the statue itself you"ll be cursed for life! Even more disturbing are reports that claim the Lady herself comes to life at night and wanders the cemetery grounds. There are many tales of visiting thrill-seekers known to run screaming from the cemetery after an encounter with the lady. However, that's not the only supernatural activity at the cemetery.

Washington Irving's Grave

Several visitors to Irving's final resting place claim they've encountered unusual spectral phenomenon. They seem to think Irving's spirit may not be "resting" at all. They describe bright orbs of light that suddenly appear in midair over the headstone. These orbs reportedly engage in a twirling dance of activity around the marker that is at times, fascinating and unnerving. The activity at Irving's grave, while unusual, is not as disturbing as the encounters with his dark creation, the Headless Horseman.

Washington Irving Gravestone Courtesy of JamesPFisherIII Creative Commons

The Headless Horseman' Ghost

Local Tarrytown legend claims that the Hessian rider that inspired Irving's tale is buried in the same cemetery. In fact, the cemetery itself has signs posted that claim the Horseman tethers his spectral steed to graves in the churchyard. Many have described seeing the so called "Galloping Hessian" searching about the cemetery for his missing head.

Headless Horseman Author's Collection

Headless Horseman Sign Sleepy Hollow Cemetery

Last Words

Sleepy Hollow Cemetery is popular, scenes from the 1970 feature film **House of Dark Shadows** were captured on camera here. The cemetery was also the filming backdrop for the Ramones music video "Pet Sematary". Literary fans may find themselves drawn to Irving's Grave. Paranormal enthusiasts might come here hoping to encounter the Bronze Lady or the Horseman himself. The cemetery is one of Tarrytown's many Historic Haunts, and one I encourage you to see for yourself.

PENNSYLVANIA

THE GHOSTS OF FARNSWORTH
Farnsworth House, Gettysburg, Pennsylvania

It's no secret that Gettysburg, Pennsylvania is thought to be among the most active paranormal locations in the world, and certainly in the U.S. The Civil War left not only tangible, but intangible effects on the area. One of the most fascinating and haunted of these locations-and one where many people claim to have encountered the intangible-is the Farnsworth House Inn.

Farnsworth House
Wikimedia Creative Commons

The History of the Farnsworth

The Farnsworth House Inn is named in memory of Elon John Farnsworth who attended the University of Michigan. In 1857 he was part of the Union Army in the capacity of forage master. He worked his way quickly up the ranks and was promoted to Captain. By the eve of the Battle of Gettysburg, President Abraham Lincoln had recommended him (in June 29, 1863) for appointment to the grade of brigadier general. Unfortunately, his appointment was not confirmed by the U.S. Senate before the Battle of Gettysburg. On July 3, 1863, Farnsworth led an ill-fated charge after Pickett's Charge failed. In that military action, he and his 65 men perished.

Before the Civil War

John F McFarlane purchased the land. It was owned previously by Reverend Alexander Dobbins sometime before 1810. The exact date is unknown. McFarlane was the first recorded owner of the home, portions of which were said to have been built in that same year in 1810.

Other parts of the structure date as far back as 1833. The house was owned by McFarlane until he died in 1851, at which point it became the property of the Bank of Gettysburg. Over the ensuing decades, it would pass through the hands of several owners.

During the time of the Battle of Gettysburg (July 1-3, 1863), it was owned by the Sweeney family. The building housed and sheltered Confederate sharpshooters. The sharpshooters used the building's height to their advantage and tried to target Federal Artillerymen.

One of the sharpshooters that stayed at the Farnsworth House is believed to have accidentally shot 20-year-old Jennie Wade, reportedly the only civilian

PENNYSLVANIA
Historic Haunts of the North II

who died during the battle. To say the building saw its share of violence from the battle is an understatement. There are over 100 bullet holes in the sides of the house. All are memories from the Civil War's deadliest battle. After the battle of Gettysburg, the house served as a hospital for wounded Confederate soldiers. Eventually the house was overrun by Union forces.

Many years after the war ended, in the early 1900s, the home was opened as a lodging house by owner George E. Black. They called the place the Sleepy Hollow Inn. It enjoyed success with its popular name, and reported involvement in the battle. Some 135 bullet holes from the battle are in the side of the house. Sometime after that, the place was renamed the Farnsworth House Inn after its namesake Union soldier. It would continue for years.

The house was purchased in 1972 by present owner Loring H. Scholtz and family. It has been restored to its former 1863 appearance. The tavern at the Inn was a frequent place of enjoyment for actors in the 1993 historical film **Gettysburg**. There are many movie props here from the award-winning film. The film's actors, like locals, tourists and journalists alike discovered how amazing the Inn's food was. Bon Appétit magazine wrote "Historic never tasted so good". I agree 100% with that statement! Farnsworth House, is still an inn and restaurant, and still has amazing food, but it is also known as a haunted hotspot in this amazing historic town.

Details of the Farnsworth Haunts

Besides being loaded with history, and having fabulous food, Farnsworth House Inn has a few haunts of its own (16 distinct ones according to the Inn's proprietors). Small wonder considering all that took place in and around the property. Among the most often encountered examples of ghostly activity, are the disembodied sounds of footsteps, and voices. In addition, cold spots are sometimes felt with no obvious source nearby to explain them. Patrons and guests of the Inn have also claimed to hear the sounds of eerie heavy breathing, and the inexplicable smell of cigar smoke (attributed by some to the spirits of highly ranking Confederate officers). The place is also noteworthy for the appearance of ghostly silhouettes that vanish quickly once seen.

It's no surprise that the apparitions of Confederate soldiers are often reported by guests and staff at the Inn. Many residual haunts have been described in the house, patrolling as if on duty, in a constant loop. Guests have even reported the sound of a "Jew's Harp" being played throughout the night, from an empty attic. Soldier's apparitions have been seen in guest rooms and even at the edge of the guest beds.

A Civil War soldier is often reportedly seen at the inn in the basement area. His apparition is accompanied by the smell of death while his spirit is present. Leading some to ask, could he be a soldier who died there on the property during the war? A ghostly Confederate sharpshooter is also sometimes seen

Farnsworth House

in the area where the bullet that struck Jennie Wade was allegedly fired.

Not all the spirits at the Inn are soldiers or military. The ghost of an eight year old boy named "Jeremy" is encountered here. The Farnsworth house collects coin donations in honor of Jeremy that are gathered and donated yearly to St. Jude's Hospital.

The phantom of a midwife has also been known to have run-ins with guests. Many have reported being startled awake by her presence as she attempts to tuck guests in. This type of turndown service is no doubt unexpected by the guests of the Inn.

Besides the midwife, another female entity who makes appearances apparently dates from the Civil War and has been described throughout the Inn by visitors. She is reported to be extremely lifelike. Many patrons have even confused her for staff.

The Sarah Black Room, and the Kitchen Spirits

Farnsworth is thought to have a great many hotspots of spiritual activity, None are more infamous than the "Sarah Black Room". Named after a family member of a previous owner; it is considered the most haunted room at the Inn. Ghostly activity and apparitions are not only frequently encountered in this room, they are often photographed. Some captured even through the window from the street below.

If the Sarah Black Room has made itself a spectral standout of the Farnsworth, the kitchen has likewise garnered attention. The spirit of a cranky cook, a woman in 19th century clothing, has been encountered looking over the products on the shelves as if deciding what to prepare. She's also seen in the hallways and the tavern, and has been reported to act rather rudely to the eatery's staff.

Final Thoughts on the Farnsworth House Inn

The Farnsworth House Inn is a fascinating place if you're a fan of paranormal activity. The spirits here tend to startle unsuspecting guests and thrill others. The Schultz family routinely encounters intense phenomenon. Enough, in fact, to promote it at the Inn and conduct their own paranormal tours on premise. This is another location featured on more than one paranormal television show, and has had activity (much of it captured on film).

Patrons at the Inn can partake in its offerings in several ways. You can stay the night here, have a fabulous meal here, or join one of their paranormal storytelling reenactments. It is definitely a "must do" if you find yourself visiting Gettysburg and is one of Historic Haunts' favorite locations. The Inn's owners are confident you'll enjoy yourself. If you're looking to encounter the paranormal, as they say, the ghosts are likely to find you!

PENNSYLVANIA
Historic Haunts of the North II

WE'RE HERE! THE PLAYFUL HAUNTS OF THE INN AT HERR RIDGE

The Inn at Herr Ridge, Gettysburg, Pennsylvania

As a fan of American History, I'm alway interested in the unexpected places it ends up taking us. At the onset of the Civil War, one little tavern was literally at the threshold of one of the biggest and bloodiest battles of the War. In short order they would find themselves pulled into the conflict, and forced to see the devastating effects of the War firsthand. Overcoming this grim and grisly environment, it has evolved to serve as a happy gathering place for the living, and also apparently, the dead.

A Place of Gathering is Created

Thomas Sweeney had an idea for a tavern and public gathering house. Sweeney located what he thought was the perfect spot. It was positioned up on a ridge, with a great view, near a major roadway (now known as Highway 30). The Sweeney Tavern and Publick House was constructed in 1815, and proved initially popular.

During the 12 years Sweeney owned the building and ran it as a Tavern, many claim that famous early 1800s bank robber, Davey Lewis, hid out here. aThey also claim he used the building's basement as a base of operations for his counterfeiting ring. Thus for a time the place was making money (literally), but it wouldn't last. By 1827, Sweeney filed for bankruptcy.

In 1828 Frederick Herr purchased the building and turned it into a "community fixture" for food, drinking, and lodging. Herr renamed the place The Herr Tavern and Publick House. Like his predecessor, Herr allegedly housed a counterfeiter as well, and laundered the money to unsuspecting travelers. The tavern was one again "making money", but this wasn't the only questionable activity going on inside. Historical records would suggest that the second floor was used as a brothel during Herr's run of the tavern.

Despite some of the less-than-honest activities going on at the tavern, the owners apparently drew the line on some things. As the Civil War approached, Herr made his Tavern available to the Underground Railroad. The approaching War that had brought escaping slaves to their doorstep, was about to come to their doorstep for real.

The Battle of Gettysburg

By the summer of 1863, the Civil War would become very real to the Herr Family. The night of June 30th, Union General John Buford's cavalry camped

PENNSYLVANIA

The Haunts of the Inn at Herr Ridge

on Herr Ridge (the land the Tavern sits on). On July 1st, muskets fired by the Confederates would push the Union troops to the outskirts of Gettysburg. The Herr Family and the Tavern's guests watched the Battle of Gettysburg from the rooftops as it played out in the fields all around them. The Herr Family and the spectators saw the wounded suddenly show up in their yard and barn. What was thought would be a minor skirmish turned out to be a costly battle.

The battle lines shifted while the conflict played out, the Tavern was suddenly on Confederate controlled property. As the bloody battle continued, the Confederates arrived and commandeered the place to serve as a field hospital. The Herr Family found themselves thrust into the unexpected role of helping surgeons, and the wounded, and feeding and caring for all.

The Tavern's four original rooms were used as impromptu operating areas. Surgeons amputated with no anesthetics or sterilized instruments. Many soldiers died here, blood soaked wooden floors were left stained, while amputated limbs were thrown out the windows to be disposed of or buried. It was a dreadful site. The smell of blood and death swept through the entire building. The Tavern stuck behind Confederate lines, ended up being used as a Confederate hospital for three days.

Herr continued to own the Tavern after the war and did his best to clean up the signs of death from the battle. However, he passed away in 1868. The Herr Family, still affected by the experience, and Herr's death, sold the building to the Read Family. Over the years, a common thread to the location, was the sudden desire its owners had to repurpose the place.

The Read Family changed the name to the Reynolds Hotel. They hoped to revamp the place to take advantage of the curious tourists coming here. These visitors wanted to see for themselves the site of the bloodiest single battle and turning point of the Civil War. The Read Family would own the hotel for several decades.

With the coming of the 1900s, the property was bought, and an attempt was made to turn it into a commercial dairy farm. It was bought and sold several more times. During these transitions it served as a music school, and rental property (last half of the 20th century).

Steve Wolf, realizing its historic value, bought the building in 1977 and restored it. Wolf became well known as a jovial and generous host. The Herr Tavern and Publick House became a very popular and public hangout in the area for drinking, food, and fun.

A huge windstorm in 1987 almost destroyed some of the older sections of the building. Wolf rebuilt, adding new touches and improvements. In 1997, Wolf put more money in the building. He built an additional wing onto the original building, added more guest rooms, and a banquet room. In 2001, Wolf bought the property next door and built an annex with additional areas to service the business.

PENNSYLVANIA
Historic Haunts of the North II

Today the place has once again changed its name. Now happily known as The Inn at Herr Ridge. It has seen some refurbishments as well. However, it still provides the amazing food, drink, and lodging Frederick Herr and Steve Wolf envisioned. It also provides visitors a glimpse into a part of the real world history of America. In addition, for some visitors, the haunted Inn at Herr Ridge provides a glimpse into the world of the paranormal as well.

The Haunts of The Inn at Herr Ridge

With as much death as the place has seen, I'm not surprised that some of the building's past is the still lingering. There are reports of paranormal activity here dating back to at least 1880. Some of this activity is common, some rather uncommon. Surprisingly, one of the building's old owners reportedly haunts the place to make sure it stays in good shape and to play host. He's such a good host that he even apparently turned the somber spirits from the Civil War into more mischievous and playful souls.

Among the "common" reports of unusual activity are cold spots, shadow figures, and strange noises. The Inn also experiences phenomenon like doors and windows opening and closing on their own, and disembodied voices. The only unpleasant or gruesome reports of activity seem to center around the window areas, where the limbs of former soldiers were tossed aside and disposed of. In these areas there have been reports of the foul smell of rotting flesh, and an overwhelming sense of sadness and negative emotions.

With its connections to the Civil War, it's no wonder that metaphysical activity at the Inn might be tied to the soldiers. Their apparitions have been spotted through the buildings and property by staff and guests. Remarkably, these soldier's spirits seem to be extremely playful and at times take great joy in startling guests and staff. Full of spectral surprises, they've been known to jiggle door handles and whisper the names of staff and guests.

They also seem to be drawn to modern conveniences and electronic devices. They're known to frequently turn televisions, fans, appliances, and modern gadgets on and off. Curious perhaps about how electric machines work (not having them in their day), they've been encountered getting into trouble in the Inn's guest rooms.

Rascally Room Activity (Especially Rooms #1-4)

The soldier's pranks are not limited to the hotel proper. They've been seen and heard making heavy footsteps just outside the doors of guests rooms (on their way in maybe). They've also been known to suddenly manifest in the rooms in front of the fireplaces, or on beds. Here they sometimes pull legs, hair, or other body parts. These bewildering "bed checks" are common.

They are particularly active in Rooms #1-4 (the Inn's "original" rooms, where the unfortunate Civil War surgeries occurred). In these rooms they fre-

PENNSYLVANIA
The Haunts of the Inn at Herr Ridge

quently move objects. Even chairs and luggage racks have been seen moving on their own. Guests in these rooms also report the sounds of their locked tight room doors opening or slamming shut. However, when those guests investigate the doors, they find them undisturbed, still locked tight.

In Room #1 candles that are blown out may suddenly reignite on their own. There's so much activity in these rooms, that the Inn keeps diaries in each. Here they encourage guests to chronicle their own encounters, and it's where visitors can read the stories of other paranormal experiences from past occupants.

Spirits Saunter Up to the Bar

According to several accounts, paranormal experiences can also be had at the bar. Here bottles have been known to move back and forth as if pushed by unseen hands. Bar occupants and their seats have also been "pushed". Hearing phantom voices at the bar is also a common event.

In fact, if asked, employees will tell a tale that occurred one day involving owner Steve Wolf and another employee. On this particular afternoon at about 2 pm, they heard the front door open and footsteps coming towards them, but no one was there and the door was locked! They looked around in disbelief. They suddenly heard a disembodied voice loudly inquire, "can I order a beer?" Wolf and the other employee just looked at each other dumbfounded.

Ruckus in the Restaurants

The bar is not the only area to have unusual activity. The Inn's restaurants have also seen their fare share of supernatural incidents. Glasses have been known to slide across tables, forks fall to the floor and stick straight in the beams, tables get messed up, and the sounds of furniture being moved in the attic above are often heard.

In the kitchen near the restaurant, a former chef once reported hearing the sounds of dishes being crashed together and broken. Upon inspection he found no broken dishes and no one else in the room. There are reports of a woman and young child in and around this room. The woman is heard singing to a crying youngster, many believe she is Frederick's wife Sarah, and the little one is their child who supposedly died of illness at a very young age.

Phantom Freddie

The last ghost thought to make an appearance is a former owner. Many of the employees have reported firsthand experiences with the ghost they call "Freddie", who they are pretty sure is Frederick Herr. Always a proud proprietor, "Freddie" seems to move objects to where he thinks they work better for

123

the establishment, or even tidy up. Maybe "Freddy" isn't happy with the look of the Tavern. Staff and guests who've encountered Freddie describe a feeling that comes over them of enthusiasm, Freddie seem to emanate a sort of encouraging atmosphere.

A Final Few Thoughts on the Herr

This pleasant and popular Inn seems to embrace its haunted heritage. They will happily share ghost stories with polite guests. Besides these everyday guests, the Inn has hosted several paranormal professionals and televised ghost hunters. More often than not they come away with strong instrument readings, unexplained evidence, or unusual encounters of their own. Psychics who visited with them or on their own, describe a sense of loss and confusion, but also a sense of playfulness.

The Inn at Herr Ridge is listed as one of the seven "Haunted Restaurants to Visit" in Gettysburg. The restaurants here have won several awards and are very popular. The Inn itself has amazing amenities (in room jacuzzi tubs in places) and boasts outstanding reviews, ratings, and landscape. I encourage my readers to check the place out. Whether you experience the paranormal while visiting The Inn at Herr Ridge or not, you are in for a "spirited experience". It is one of the most haunted hotspots in Northeast Gettysburg with amazing drinks and food. What a great Historic Haunt.

THE TICKING TOMB
Landenberg, Pennsylvania

"And have I not told you that what you mistake for madness is but over-acuteness of the sense? --now, I say, there came to my ears a low, dull, quick sound, such as a watch makes when enveloped in cotton. I knew that sound well, too. It was the beating of the old man's heart. It increased my fury, as the beating of a drum stimulates the soldier into courage."
— Edgar Allan Poe, "The Tell-Tale Heart and Other Writings"

In the small community of Landenberg, Pennsylvania in Southern Chester County, there's a historic graveyard with a unique claim to fame. This place of eternal rest boasts a grave that has only grown more famous with the passing of time. The tomb is not only connected to the famed early Americans Charles Mason and Jeremiah Dixon, but also reportedly to the master poet and storyteller Edgar Allan Poe. The mysterious tomb also reportedly ticks, like a watch. How is that possible you ask, well for that story we'll have to turn back time a bit.

Turning Back the Clock for a Bit of History

In 1764, Jeremiah Dixon and Charles Mason (surveyors and creators of the Mason Dixon line) established a headquarters at Newark's, St. Patrick's Tavern. This tavern was once reportedly located for many years about nine miles away on or near the site of the present day Deer Park Tavern in Delaware (see the story in my first **Historic Haunts of the North** book). The two men were reportedly sent out to survey and mark definitively the boundaries between the colonies of Pennsylvania and Maryland. Several colonists felt they may have been paying extra taxes for overlapping territories. Maps of the day were inaccurate.

Mason was an inventor and mathematician. He entered a contest (sponsored by the British Parliament) to develop a chronometer which could accurately measure longitude at sea. For the winner, the prize was some 20,000 pounds sterling (approximately 3.5 million sterling today, or about $4.6 million in U.S. Dollars). In the mid 1700s, there were very few portable watches or chronometers, especially anything close to pocket size. Mason had reportedly succeeded in creating a reliable working device.

Timekeepers of the era courtesy Jordiferrer Creativ Commons

Mason traveled to Landenberg, Pennsylvania to set up his own tent amidst a surveyor's tent city. There he sought to barter for supplies. A fishwife's son,

125

a toddler named Fithian Minuit, wandered into Mason's tent. The child was known to try to eat everything he touched and so he swallowed Mason's invention. Amazingly, the device continued to tick in the young boy's stomach. While many hoped he would pass the device, alas it was not to be, and the device remained in the child's stomach. The furious Mason was said to have cursed the boy, *"May my creation function until the end of time, proof that I would have won the celebrated prize."*

Years passed and the boy grew into a man. Interestingly, he became a clockmaster. Minuit met a sea captain who needed his broken chronometer repaired. He fixed the man's device and struck up a friendship with the captain. The captain asked Minuit to take care of his daughter Martha if any harm should befall him while at sea. Minuit agreed. Unfortunately, the prophetic captain was lost at sea within a year of their agreement. Minuit, in keeping with his promise, married the captain's daughter who he'd fallen in love with.

Minuit (whose name means midnight in French), would reportedly consider Martha the love of his life. His bride-to-be learned of the steady ticking in his chest. The two agreed the ticking would come to symbolize their love for each other, a reminder perhaps to spend precious time together. The pair reportedly lived a very happy life together. Martha would enjoy 40 years of marriage to Minuit before passing. Her husband lived to be almost 80. He reportedly died at the gravesite of his beloved wife. His body was discovered by a group of men who were hunting in the area. When they both had passed, they were buried side by side. Minuit's chronometer apparently continued to tick away, a reminder of their eternal love.

The Tell-Tale Poet

It has been suggested that Edgar Allen Poe may have visited the grave while staying at the nearby Deer Park Tavern in Newark (again check out the story in my previous North book), and found the inspiration for his short story "The Tell-Tale Heart". Mason and Dixon stayed at the same tavern nearly a century before, and Poe could have easily heard the tale there.

It's High Time for My Last Thoughts

Most researchers agree that there is an underground spring that seem to run below the cemetery and may account for the ticking sound. However, that spring has reportedly rerouted since and this may provide an answer to the lack of ticking from Minuit's grave marker. Many claim they can still hear the ticking even without the stream. This would suggest a more supernatural reason for the ticking tomb. Admittedly, the cemetery exhibits an eerie quality already that's only enhanced by this local legend. I haven't had a chance to investigate this Historic Haunt myself, but maybe it's about time I did!

RHODE ISLAND

THE GHOST OF THE SWAMP BRIDE
The Swamp Bride at Maureen Circle, Burrillville Rhode Island

I've encountered many legendary local ghost stories in my travels, but few as heart-wrenching as the tale of a tragic couple in Burrillville, Rhode Island. This area itself has a history. The region now considered Mapleville, was once North Gloucester and thought to be settled as far back as 1662. John Smith was thought to be among the early settlers. It was named after James Burrell Jr a U.S. Senator. Today, most know it as a setting with beautiful and idyllic landscapes. Unfortunately, it's also the site of the most noteworthy of the many ghost tales of Rhode Island.

Love at Last

The story starts with the suggestion that two people, Katherine Donahue and Jonathon Cuttle, were completely in love with each other and were engaged to be married. They had happily found each other and were ecstatically planning their upcoming nuptials. Jonathan was a farmer and had a farm on the outskirts of town. Katherine lived with her brother Charles and the family at Donahue homestead, not too far from the swamp. Katherine was something of a catch and turned down other suitors before meeting and being courted by Jonathan. Among those who sought her hand unsuccessfully was a neighbor named David Jones. He too was madly in love with Katherine but as we already know her heart belonged to Jonathon. David was furious over the couple's upcoming marriage and decided if he couldn't have Katherine, no one would.

One day, sometime in August, between 1806-1810 (details vary by source) and one month before the wedding; David left his house knife in hand determined to do something about it. He headed for the farm of Jonathan Cuttle. When David arrived on the farm he spied Jonathan and waited for his best chance to strike. That moment came when Jonathan, who was moving hay with a pitchfork, set it aside to take a break. David seized the pitchfork and used it to stab Jonathan through the back. Then he headed to see Katherine.

Katherine had gone to an area near the swamp to collect water for the family while her brother Charles hunted pheasants nearby for dinner. David came upon Katherine sitting blissfully unaware by the water's edge. He threw his knife, striking her in the neck. She fell sideways screaming in horrific pain before succumbing to her wound. The screaming drew the attention of her brother who ran furiously to his sister's side only to discover he was too late and she was dead. The details of what happened next are as sketchy as the

RHODE ISLAND
Historic Haunts of the North II

exact date of the incident, perhaps the lack of record keeping at the time. What is certain to generations of people in the area is that this part of Burrillville is haunted!

Tales of the Paranormal and the "Swamp Bride"

Needless to say, Katherine's love story turned gory in a short period of time and the area where this tragedy took place is reportedly extremely active. Reports of strange sounds in the area are plentiful. Most claim the horrific screams can still be heard around the time of the murder. It seems as though the murder is still taking place year after year around the time which it originally occurred.

The area is now more fully developed than it was in Katherine's time and several additional houses have sprung up in the region. Residents of these houses have frequently reported paranormal activity, describing disembodied footsteps, eerie voices, and whispers. They also mention the fact that their rocking chairs frequently rock on their own accord, with no wind or anyone sitting in them.

Katherine's apparition is also said to be seen, typically in a long gown that appears to be wet and dirty. She is often seen coming from the woods and appears to have just crawled out of the swamp. This has earned her spirit the nickname "The Swamp Bride". Jonathon's ghost has been reported as well, but not with the same frequency. The spirits of the unfortunate star-crossed lovers are said to vanish into thin air if anyone approaches or tries to interact with them.

If you find yourself in rural northern Rhode Island you'll be amazed by the beauty of the surrounding flora and fauna. If you travel to Maureen Circle you may be amazed by other sights, perhaps that of Katherine's ghost itself. The tale of the Swamp Bride is known throughout this National Heritage Corridor, to us it is one of the saddest Historic Haunts.

RHODE ISLAND

SPIRITS, AND A MASTER OF HORROR OR TWO, AT SWAN POINT CEMETERY
Swan Point Cemetery, Providence, Rhode Island

"The oldest and strongest emotion of mankind is fear, and the oldest and strongest kind of fear is fear of the unknown"
— H.P. Lovecraft, **Supernatural Horror in Literature**

If you travel to Providence, Rhode Island you will discover a very prominent rural cemetery on Blackstone Boulevard. This historic cemetery, Swan Point Cemetery by name, is well known for its tranquil landscapes, and scenic greenspace, especially to local residents and hikers and bikers. It's also well known for the abundance of well known and celebrated citizens interred here. To fans of the paranormal and creative writing, it holds special distinction. Swan Point Cemetery is reportedly haunted by two particular spirits, both known to be masters of literary horror.

*Swan Point Cemetery
Kenneth C. Zirkel
Wikimedia Creative Commons*

Swan Point Cemetery

In the early 19th century residents of Rhode Island had the idea to create a burial place that was modeled after Victorian cemeteries. They hoped to create a place with scenic parks, benches, pathways, and even picnic grounds. Their vision was realized when Swan Point Cemetery was established in 1846. It originally consisted of 60 acres, with approximately 40,000 internments. In 1858 a new charter was developed to make the cemetery non-profit. It was later taken over by the Proprietors of Swan Point Cemetery.

Swan Point Cemetery boasts a remarkable number of notable burial sites. Among them are some 23 Governors of the state, and a vast amount of local and national politicians. It also contains the graves of olympic athletes, medal-of-honor winners, famous painters, journalists and philanthropists. Visitors may also discover that famous inventors are interred here, including George Henry Carliss (Carliss Steam Engine), and George Coby (waterproof concrete, construction grade glass bricks, first electrical Christmas tree lights). However, one of the most well known souls to be buried here is the author H.P. Lovecraft.

Lovecraft is considered by many to be a master of horror. He is mentioned in the same vein as Edgar Allan Poe (one of his heroes and mine). So let's

129

RHODE ISLAND
Historic Haunts of the North II

take a closer look at one of the most famous and controversial dark story writers in history.

The Coming of H.P. Lovecraft

Howard Phillips (H.P.) Lovecraft was born in Providence, Rhode Island on August 20th of 1890. Lovecraft's father was institutionalized not long after he was born in 1893 for mental health issues (something Lovecraft would fear throughout his life). This forced his mother to take him and move in with his wealthy maternal grandparents and aunts. Lovecraft was a remarkably intelligent child, a prodigy perhaps, who was reportedly repeating poetry at 2, reading and writing at 3, and had read the complete Arabian Nights stories by the age of 5.

H.P. Lovecraft
Public Domain

Lovecraft's grandfather, Whipple Van Buren Phillips, was a very successful businessman (he owned most of the land in Greene, Rhode Island). He took notice of his grandson's amazing mind and nurtured him, encouraging him to read and appreciate classical literature and English poetry. He also pushed him to write, including corresponding with him when out of town on business.

Unfortunately, Lovecraft's grandmother Robie died in 1896. Lovecraft would later remark that his grandmother's death sent the family into a "gloom from which they would never recover". After her death, Lovecraft's mother and aunts wore black mourning dresses appropriate for the time, that he claimed "horrified" him. Something about these ornate dresses inspired nightmares in the young man (he would later tap these bad dreams to craft his "night-gaunts", creatures seen in some of his darker works).

Lovecraft had bouts of sickness growing up and moments described as "nervous breakdowns". He also suffered severe social anxiety and agoraphobia (a fear of open or closed spaces that might cause you to panic or have feelings of being helpless or embarrassed). This caused the youth to retreat from contact with others and read even more voraciously. Among his favorite books were those concerning science and astronomy, horror fiction, and mythology. He would later inject all of these into his stories. As adulthood approached, he seemed to show signs of psychological breakdown himself and may have developed xenophobia (fear or dislike of something foreign or strange).

Lovecraft began to write short stories at this time. In the spring of 1904, he wrote the first draft of "The Beast in the Cove" (it was finished in 1905 when he was 15). As Spring progressed that year, Lovecraft's grandfather passed away, leaving the family an inheritance. Years later Lovecraft would include a character remarkable similar to his grandfather in his semi-autobiographical novella "The Dunwich Horror". His grandfather's and mentor's death defi-

RHODE ISLAND
Swan Point Cemetery

nitely affected the young man. At around this time he became more intrigued with darker stories, particularly those written by Mary Shelley and Edgar Allan Poe (his favorite).

   Lovecraft greatly admired Poe, and would mention Poe multiple times during his life in essays, poems, letters, and lectures. In fact, he once wrote, " When I write-stories, Edgar Allan Poe is my model." Lovecraft would borrow concepts of psychology pioneered by Poe in his characters and blend it with dread, curiosity, and horror. Poe created the detective genre with his character C. Auguste Dupin in "The Murders in the Rue Morgue".

   Lovecraft would duplicate the concept with many if his characters in stories like "The Tomb" (which he wrote after visiting a relative's grave in Swan Point Cemetery), "The Outsider", and "The Horror of Red Hook" (whose main character was a detective with the NYPD), among others. Unlike Poe's detective, Lovecraft's protagonists often stumble (unbeknownst to them), into a world of dark supernatural forces. These details became part of many of Lovecraft's stories and his "world view". In some stories he included darker elements of the supernatural, like lurking subterranean creatures, ancestral curses, tentacled monsters, and old ancient gods and powerful beings not originally of this world. Nowhere is this more evident than in his most famous creation "Cthulhu"

The Spawning of Cthulhu

   In many of his stories Lovecraft presented narrators who told the stories of the "Great Old Ones" (sometimes called Elder Gods). These God-like creatures came to Earth from space and once ruled the planet. They were, at one time, revered by early humans. Many of these ancient ones lie dormant, awaiting the time when they will rise again (anybody else thinking of **Ghost Busters**). The most famous of these was Cthulhu.

Weird Tales featuring "The Call of Cthulhu" Public Domain

   Cthulhu was introduced in Lovecraft's short story "The Call of Cthulhu". Cthulhu was a great terrifying monster. He was referred to as "The Dread One" and "He who is not to be named" (Potter fans might notice the influence). Cthulhu resembled a giant dragon-like cephalopod. He looked like a green octopus in parts with a rubbery-looking body, leathery wings, claws on his hands and forefeet, and a face of full of tentacled feelers (Pirates of the Caribbean fans may see similarities).

   The Elder-God Cthulhu hibernated ominously in the depths of the ocean, waiting to unleash untold horrors. Cthulhu or his minions would sometimes rise if called upon or disturbed. These horrors could infiltrate your mind

131

RHODE ISLAND
Historic Haunts of the North II

(among other things) and drive you crazy. Most of Lovecraft's narrators encountering Cthulhu or other creatures from their pantheon, went mad!

Lovecraft's Belated Success

Lovecraft's dark stories and masterful writing technique took some time to connect with the general public. Instead of choosing more traditional literary mediums to get his work published, he worked in the niche, speculative fiction world of mass market pulp fiction. Lovecraft became one of the more popular of the pulp "zine" writers, and along with future greats like Ray Bradbury, helped create a genre called "Weird Fiction" (named after the popular Weird Tales zine). These pulp sources gave us iconic characters like **Conan the Barbarian**, **Tarzan**, **Flash Gordon**, and **Buck Rogers**, among others.

Besides his writing prowess, and invented myths, Lovecraft's popularity was built upon his insistence to let others "play in his sandbox". He created fictional settings for stories, typically in New England, like Arkham, Massachusetts, and Miskatonic University (the place where powerful occult books were kept and studied). This included Lovecraft's Necronomicon, the Book of the Dead (shout out to ***Evil Dead*** and "Ash" fans out there). These fictional settings were sometimes collectively called "Lovecraft Country". Lovecraft encouraged and gave permission to other writers, and fan fiction makers, to utilize his settings, or remix and cross elements. This, in turn, helped build the popularity of the communal reality often called "Cthulhu Mythos".

The End of Lovecraft's Life and His Complicated Legacy

Lovecraft's mother would start to suffer mental problems and be institutionalized in 1919. His family would squander their fortune. He was forced to leave the family estate. He moved briefly to New York. However, New York took a toll on his mental health and finances, and he returned to Providence in 1926. Unfortunately, he died penniless and unknown in 1937. Swan Point Cemetery is where his eternal resting place is. Lovecraft's works never saw popularity or commercial success while he was alive. Sadly, like many creatives, Lovecraft would achieve great recognition posthumously.

His talented genius for writing has led most scholars to consider him one of the most significant horror writers of the 20th century. While Edgar Allan Poe is considered the "Father of Gothic Horror", Lovecraft is considered to be the "Father of Cosmic Horror". His influence on writing and popular culture is immense and undeniable. His written works and themes saturate modern horror and literary fiction.

Lovecraft has reportedly influenced Stephen King. H.R. Giger's Alien designs, and many others. Science has even named spiders and sea creatures after his famous creation, Cthulhu. Lovecraft has had a huge resurgence that began in the early 1980s, when some of his stories and themes were adapted and presented in film and fiction. Modern writer's works, dabbling in similar themes and ideas, are often called "Lovecraftian Horror".

Unfortunately, Lovecraft has a very tainted legacy. Influenced, it seems, by his many fears and beliefs. His characters, looking for the causes of the terrible evils they were facing, often blamed them on specific ethnic groups or made racist metaphors. In certain cases, Lovecraft himself made literal racist comments. He also included and justified racist police violence and white supremacy in some stories and featured them in a positive, supportive light (especially in his own personal correspondences). Horror and fantasy fans, and writers, have had trouble trying to come to terms with this. I must admit, before I researched this entry, I knew "of" Lovecraft (as I do several authors who dabble in supernatural stories and themes), but I was not, and am not a fan.

Despite these uncomfortable elements, Lovecraft has a very devoted fan base. His more rabid fans are collectively known as "Cthooligans". In 1977, a group of his loyal fans raised money to buy him a headstone of his own at Swan Point Cemetery. On this headstone they had inscribed Lovecraft's name, birth and death dates, and the phrase " I AM PROVIDENCE" - a line from one of his personal letters.

Back to Swan Point Cemetery

Lovecraft and I do share a love of Edgar Allan Poe, and interestingly, Poe has a connection to the cemetery beyond Lovecraft. In his later life, Poe became smitten from a distance with poet, activist, and intellectual, Sarah Helen Whitman (Whitman is interred in another nearby Providence Cemetery, North Burial Ground). The two met in person in September of 1848. Poe courted her, and they had many long conversations and walks through the scenic Swan Point Cemetery. In fact, it's where he proposed to her. Alas, it was not meant to be, as Poe passed (for more on Poe's last few days check out ***Historic Haunts of the North*** and the story on Edgar Allan Poe's Gravesite).

Swan Point Cemetery Today

Despite its many older "residents", Swan Point has adapted fully to these modern times. The cemetery occupants and grave markers have been included in the computer for over 20 years. They're even accessible by QR code.

They're also early adapters, embracing some eco-friendly ideas. They compost old floral arrangements and use them to help grow new flowers in an on-site greenhouse. They've also added a cremation garden.

Swan Point is considered by many to be one of the most prestigious burial grounds in Rhode Island. It's known to be one of the most picturesque and beautiful cemeteries in the nation and the world. It's also known to be haunted!

The Spirits of Swan Point

There are numerous reports of paranormal activity in this scenic cemetery. Enough for it to be included in local ghost tours and magazine and newspaper stories. It's also mentioned in books (like this one) that recount tales of the paranormal in New England. Many of these include the more common incidents of eerie sensations, disembodied sounds, and ghostly apparitions. Some of these apparitions are more frequently reported than others, and among these is the ghost of Sullivan Ballou.

Sullivan's History, Correspondence, and Spirit

Sullivan Ballou was a lawyer, and later politician from Rhode Island. He was a staunch supporter of Abraham Lincoln and became an officer in the Union Army. Unfortunately, his career didn't last long. While a combatant during the Confederate attack at Bull Run. he was hit by a cannonball. This cannonball tore off part of his right leg, and also killed his horse. Ballou was carried off the field. The rest of his leg was amputated. He died from his wounds a week later and was buried in Sudley Church's graveyard.

Sadly, his story didn't end with his corpse, it continued. The Confederate forces that controlled the region, allegedly exhumed his body, decapitated it, and burned it. Ballou's body was never recovered. Charred bone and ash were reburied in Swan Point Cemetery. His wife Sarah is buried next to her husband's recovered remains.

Ballou would become famous for a letter he wrote to Sarah and their two kids, sensing his demise. This letter was found undelivered, in his trunk after he passed. It was personally delivered to his widow by William Sprague, then Governor of Rhode Island. This letter, was featured prominently in the award winning documentary, **The Civil War**, by Ken Burns. These excerpts from the letter might explain Ballou's undying love for his darling wife and kids, and perhaps why his spirit may have returned.

"...Sarah, my love for you is deathless, it seems to bind me to you with mighty cables that nothing but Omnipotence could break; and yet my love of Country comes over me like a strong wind and bears me irresistibly on with all these chains to the battlefield.
...Forgive my many faults, and the many pains I have caused you. How thoughtless and foolish I have often been! How gladly would I wash out with my tears every little spot upon your happiness, and struggle with all the misfortune of this world, to shield you and my children from harm. But I cannot.

RHODE ISLAND
Swan Point Cemetery

I must watch you from the spirit land and hover near you, while you buffet the storms with your precious little freight, and wait with sad patience till we meet to part no more.

But, O Sarah! If the dead can come back to this earth and flit unseen around those they loved, I shall always be near you; in the brightest day and in the darkest night—amidst your happiest scenes and gloomiest hours—always, always; and if there be a soft breeze upon your cheek, it shall be my breath; or the cool air fans your throbbing temple, it shall be my spirit passing by. "

—excerpt from Ballou's letter, featured in ***The Civil War***

This powerful letter resonated with many who feel deep emotion for their loved ones. It has inspired songs, stories, quests in video games, and perhaps Ballou's spirit to return. There have been several reports that would suggest his spirit roams Swan Point. There are even reports of a man in a period-esque black coat seen visiting and strolling through the cemetery with an adoring female spirit. Romantics like to speculate that this might be Ballou and his wife reunited, but there are other identities suggested for this ghostly pair.

Sprague's Spirit

Another haunt of Swan Point that has been supposedly identified by eyewitnesses is connected to Governor William Sprague, who delivered Ballou's letter. Sprague and his brother Amasa were members of a wealthy cotton making family in Rhode Island. They were educated at the Irving Institute in Tarrytown, New York (find out more about Tarrytown and the Headless Horseman's ghost in my Washington Irving Sunnyside entry in ***Historic Haunts of the North***). Unlike his brother William, Amasa was reportedly an unpleasant man, prone to violence. In fact, the whole family had a reputation for it. They used their considerable influence in the area at times to torment and harass others, and as a result were supposedly cursed. The family was reportedly plagued by the ghosts of victims they wronged. Sprague family members tended to die by suicide, or were killed in violent confrontations. Amasa would follow suit. His body was found beaten and shot. His restless apparition has been seen making its way through the gravestones at Swan Point.

Spectral Sideburns

Amasa's brother, the previously mentioned William, served in the Civil War under General Ambrose Evers Burnside. Burnside was known for two things. The first being extremely unlucky in battle, with women, and in business. The other was his spectacular growth of whiskers which became known as "sideburns", a reversal

Ambrose Burnside
Public Domain

RHODE ISLAND
Historic Haunts of the North II

of parts of his name, and a permanent part of American vernacular.

Before the Civil War, Burnside was engaged to Charlotte "Lottie" Moon. Upon the day of their marriage, when the minister asked if she would take him for her husband, she reportedly shouted " No Siree Bob!" before running out and leaving him at the altar. Her phrase has also become part of American vernacular. Burnside would later arrest her after it was discovered she was engaged in espionage for the Confederacy during the Civil War.

Burnside's service in the military was equally disastrous. He had the unfortunate luck of serving under bad commanders, given impossible situations, and unrealistic missions. He was eventually relieved of command.

In civilian life he invented several infantry aiding devices. The rights to his most prominent, the cavalry firearm, were robbed and taken from him. He died in 1881. He is buried in Swan Point.

His ghost has been seen wandering the cemetery. His spectral sideburns making his spirit easy to identify. His purpose for haunting the cemetery is unknown.

Other Ghosts of Swan Point

There are many other metaphysical manifestations reported at the cemetery. Including Thomas Dorr, who led a rebellion to fight for democracy and electoral and voting reforms. However, it's the last two reports of apparitions I want to mention that have captured the imagination of the general public, ghost tours, and literary and paranormal enthusiasts.

The Poe-tential Couple's Amorous Apparitions

We've previously mentioned the ghost of the loving couple seen strolling through Swan Point. As I stated many romantics suggest these wandering phantoms are the happily reunited ghosts of Sullivan Ballou and his wife. Others (including myself and ghost tour guides in the area), have a d different view. The distinctive black coat and manner of the gentleman's ghost as he strolls insubstantial through the cemetery ground with his lady suggest to some, the spirits of Edgar Allan Poe and his fiancee Sarah Helen Whitman.

The decscription given of this ghost more closely resembles the "Father of Gothic Horror". In addition, the female spirit seems to more closely resemble the object of his affection, Sarah Helen Whitman. Another reason eyewitnesses have assigned this male spirit to be Poe, is that it has also been encountered alone, making his way down Benefit Street at dusk, in the general direction of Whitman's former residence.

H.P. Lovecraft

The last and most popular phantom encountered in Swan Point is H.P. Lovecraft. The devoted Poe fan's gravesite is one of the most popular in the cemetery, and one where many unusual accounts of paranormal phenomenon seem to occur. Lovecraft was a master writer of horror so it's no wonder that his grave gets a lot of attention. Many believe his ghost haunts the cemetery and more frequently, his grave site.

On March 15 every year an annual tribute is held around the time of his death by his fans in hopes of connecting with Lovecraft's spirit. It is believed by many that his apparition or ghost appears every year to attend the festivities. Reports of his spirit manifesting not only attest to this, but the weird activity centered around his grave that seems like something right out of his "Weird Fiction".

One year attendees to this gathering swore they heard a disembodied cackling at the time they tried to connect with him. On another anniversary, a freak isolated atmospheric condition created a "snow shower" where it started to snow suddenly as the group gathered and tried to contact Lovecraft's spirit, but only around the area of his grave. It seems as though something strange happens almost every year they tried to make contact with the deceased author. Lovecraft fans leave tokens at his gravesite during these get togethers, often connected to his stories.

Now it seems Lovecraft fans have tried to organize the gathering in April hoping for warmer weather (the average temperature in Providence in Mid March is between 29 and 45 degree), However, the activity has declined drastically. Connecting well with the author's spirit doesn't seem to occur on the the later date.

Some Last Words About Swan Point

Swan Point Cemetery is remarkable. Its history dates back to 1722. It is one of the country's first rural cemeteries, and is one of the world's most notable garden cemeteries.

The gorgeous blossoming trees and flowers, and richly detailed, sculptural gravesite are unlike anything anywhere else. It is a joy to stroll through for nature lovers, casual observers, and "taphophiles" (people interested in cemeteries, funerals, and gravesites). The Cemetery is so beautiful that the Butler Avenue Trolley was routed here decades ago for locals to come and walk the grounds.

Many who come here are surprised to discover the beauty of the place, and the strolling spirits of its buried residents. Poe's spirit alone would draw many fans of the paranormal. but add H.P. Lovecraft and the others and this is a powerful Historic Haunt.

In 1977, it was added to the National Register of Historic Places. It is one of the two largest cemeteries in Providence. I encourage my readers to check this active and picturesque place out for themselves.

VERMONT

THE HAUNTING STORY OF THE HARTFORD BRIDGE DISASTER
Hartford, Vermont

On a cold day in February, 1887 in Hartford Vermont, a tragic accident would occur that would forever change the course of train safety. The accident would be considered the worst railroad disaster in Vermont railroading history. It would forever leave its mark on this area, in a real and spiritual way.

The Montreal Express

In the early morning hours of a cold winter day in February, **The Montréal Express** was on its way to its namesake city. The veteran crew had a combined decades worth of railway experience. The train had come from Boston and it pulled out of the station at 2:10am, 90 minutes behind schedule. seventy-seven passengers were on board most headed north to Montréal's Winter Carnival. In addition to the passengers, some twelve or so crew were on board.

Among the passengers and crew was Henry Tewksbury, a well known lecturer who had just come home from giving a lecture on Gettysburg. He came from White River Junction and was hoping to join his friend Smith Sturtevant, a Civil War veteran who attended his lecture, and coincidentally, was the conductor of the Montréal Express. They were joined by David and Joseph Maigret, a father and son who were traveling back to their home in Quebec. George Parker was also on hand in his capacity of breakman of the train.

Wrong Place Wrong Time the Tragedy Unfolds

Ten minutes after leaving White River Junction, the train was steaming towards a bridge near West Hartford. The Montréal Express had no clue what it was heading towards that cold winter day in February. Unseen, a broken rail in the railroad tracks up ahead would be the end of the line for part of the train.

On board Tewksbury felt the train excessively jolt and the cars sway back and forth, which to him meant it was about to derail. This realization was also made by breakman George Parker, who looked toward the rear of the train and recognized it was about to jump the tracks. Parker grabbed a lantern and jumped from the train into deep snow and ultimately ended up near the frozen White River below.

VERMONT
The Hartfrd Bridge Disaster

The rear sleeper car fitfully wrestled free of the tracks flipping and plummeting towards the river forty feet below and taking a string of train cars off the track with it. The connectors of the train, unable to handle the strain, snapped, sparing the locamotive and the mail car. The plumeting train cars struck thick ice and the weight of the heavy train wheels shattered and splintered large sections of the wooden cars. This instantly killed many passengers, and the wreckage pinned others. To make matters worse, the train's whale oil karosean lamps and coal stores soon ignited the draperies, upholstries, and wood of the cars themselves. Creating an inferno.

Hartford Bridge Disaster photograph in Public Domain

Among the pinned passengers was Tewksbury, he was eventually painfully pulled free by crew members and injured survivors. Tewksbury was placed by a stone support beam near the bridge and worried in horror as his friend Sturtevant, the conductor crawled through a car with his clothing a blaze. Rescuers quickly moved to shovel snow on the conductor and put out the flames. Badly burned, he would later die at a nearby farmhouse with his friend by his side.

In another nearby section of the wreckage David Maigret also found himself pinned and unable to escape. David could feel the heat of the approaching blaze and had just enough time to say his goodbyes to his son, handing him his watch and pocket book. His son, Joseph, not pinned, watched in horror as the flames engulfed his father as he escaped the train car.

As all of these unfortunate events played out, breakman Parker borrowed horses from nearby farms to get help and secure rescuers. Pingree House and Paine Farm at opposite ends of the bridge very quickly became hospitals, recovery rooms, and morgues. In short order, survivors of the train accident, were faced with -20 ° F temperatures and the need to move as the bridge itself eventually collapsed.

When all was said and done 37 passengers and crew were dead, victims of the crash and the fire that followed, or swept away and drowned by icy river currents. In some cases people had to be identified by bits and pieces and in at least one unfortunate case a parent and child were fused together by fire. Additionally fifty others were injured.

On February 5th, 1887, according to the Vermont Historical Society, Professor Robert Fletcher, Dean of Dartmouth College's Thayer School of Engineering, was assigned to lead an independent investigation of the crash aided by a handful of his students. He determined the cause of the wreck was not human error, but a defective rail caused perhaps by the elements or other outside factors. Newspapers would describe the accident site using descrip-

VERMONT
Historic Haunts of the North II

tions reminiscent of today's horrific airplane crashes, but on ice. They would claim that the Montreal Express was merely at the quote "wrong place at the wrong time".

The accident and the horrific details described by the press led congress and state legislatures to act quickly to improve train safety passing the "Railroad Appliance Act". Eventually the Hartford Bridge was rebuilt. The new bridge and tracks are steel and much safer than they were in 1887. However, the spot still apparently holds some strong residual energy from the tragic events.

The Haunts of the Hartford Bridge

Many people passing through and exploring the site have reported the smell of a fire as if something were burning. There have even been reports of witnesses feeling the heat from this supernatural fire. Investigators to the area quickly discover there were no recent fires or even remnants of something that had recently burned.

Besides the reports of ethereal flames and heat, there have been numerous reports of disembodied voices wailing in pain and calling for help. These reports aren't limited to the site of the disaster. Similar encounters have occurred and been reported by witnesses who visited the Paine farm which once housed victims (especially the barn) and still stands . Paranormal activity reported in the area also includes eyewitnesses to several apparitions.

The Maigret Ghosts and Others

Many believe one of the spirits haunting here is that of a young boy named Joseph Maigret and his father who died in the accident. The apparitions of both have both seen in late 19th-century clothing, near the river banks of the crash site. They appear to be in distress and soaked from head to toe. When people try to approach them and assist, they disappear. Joseph's ghost has also been encountered by passing drivers before vanishing into thin air as they pass.

Apparitions have also been reported of a ghostly railway worker. Some have suggested this could be Sturtevant's ghost. He reportedly patrols the road and nearby rail area hoping to prevent another accident.

Final Thoughts

The Hartford Bridge disaster should never be forgotten. It seems the tragic accident has left a strong residual energy on the area, which often happens when something traumatic thing takes place. This story remains one of Vermont's, and indeed one of the more unfortunate Historic Haunts.

WASHINGTON D.C.

THE EXORCIST STEPS
Corner of Prospect Street and 76th Street NW, Georgetown University, Washington DC

Deep in the heart of the Old Georgetown Historic District of Georgetown University, you will find a set of steps. While there are many steps on the campus of this prestigious university, this flight of steps is unique. The stairs descend from the corner of Prospect Street and 76th Street NW. They lead down to a small parking lot called the "Car Barn".

These concrete steps were an iconic part of the most popular horror movie of it's time, and perhaps of all time. Because of the success of this horror masterpiece, the steps have become known worldwide. They are forever connected to the supernatural because of the book and film they're featured in **The Exorcist**. They're also thought by some to be haunted.

The Exorcist Steps courtesy of Dmitri K Wikimedia Creative Commons

Georgetown University and the Famous Steps

Georgetown College/University was established January 23rd, 1789. It is a private research university in the Georgetown neighborhood of Washington DC. It is home to the country's largest student run business, largest student run financial institute, and has the oldest continuously run student theatre troupe.

The University has seen its fair share of history and history makers. It's also educated its fair share of famous authors including Sinclair Lewis (**Main Street**), and Roald Dahl (**Charlie and the Chocolate Factory**). In the late 40s a young writer named William Peter Blatty was attending the school. While there he happened to read a story in The Washington Post about a real-life exorcism performed on a 14 year old boy (a supposed student of the University). The exorcism was performed in Maryland and the boy was reportedly brought to Georgetown for treatment. The story had a huge impact on Blatty, and would be a first step in his climb to achieve a career as a well known author.

In 1971, Blatty released his novel The Exorcist, which was inspired by the article he'd read as a student at Georgetown before his graduation in 1950. The book chronicled the story of a young girl named Regan, possessed by a demon, and her mother's attempt to rescue her via exorcism by two Catholic Priests. The book became wildly successful and plans were made to make a

141

WASHINGTON D.C.
Historic Haunts of the North II

movie from it.

Blatty was the screenwriter and producer, he was joined by William Friedkin, director of **The French Connection**. The crew came to film at Georgetown. Many Hoya Students were extras in the film and many scenes were filmed in and around campus. Early in the movie the character of Burke Dennings is killed by the demon possessing Regan, and thrown out her window down these steps where his body is found and the death is ruled an accident. During the climactic final scenes of the movie, the steps are seen again. One of the two exorcising priests, Father Karras, saves the young girl Regan by encouraging the demon that has taken hold of her to possess him instead. The demon obliges and the priest jumps out the window falling down the stone steps. He is give last rites and dies.

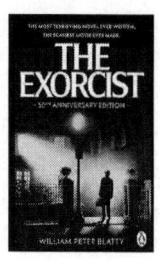

The Exorcist Author's Collection

This now famous flight of stairs at the University made an impression on Blatty as a student (enough to feature them in the book and movie) and was another step in his ascent to success. **The Exorcist** was released on December 26, 1973. It was a huge commercial success. For his efforts, Blatty won an Academy Award for Best Screenplay. Since then the movie and the steps have achieved legendary status.

More About the Steps and Exorcist Day

The steps were once referred to as "M Street Steps" for the shortcut they provided Georgetown students between M and Prospect Streets. They had previously been known as "Hitchcock Steps" in honor of the late Alfred Hitchcock (another master of suspense known for his horror film **Psycho** which to many people was the best horror movie in the world until **The Exorcist**). After the movie, this flight of steps would forever be known as "The Exorcist Steps".

Coincidentally, **The Exorcist's** author, Blatty, lived in Georgetown in the late 1970s, four houses down from the steps he knew so well. On Halloween Weekend of 2015, Washington D.C. and Georgetown celebrated "Exorcist Day". The stairs were officially recognized (with a plaque unveiled at the base of the steps) as a D.C. Landmark and official tourist destination. The film's director Friedkin joined author and Georgetown alum Blatty at the ceremony. Today people from all over the world take pictures at the iconic steps. Many of them have claimed there's a supernatural connection that goes beyond the film.

The Exorcist Steps Plaque courtesy APK Wikimedia Creative Commons

142

WASHINGTON D.C.
The Exorcist Steps

A Haunted Production

The filming problems experienced during the making of **The Exorcist** are legendary. The filmmakers experienced: fires (that burned whole sets down), weird accidents, unusual injuries and deaths (to some of the cast and crew and their relations). These led the Professor of Theology at Georgetown to bless the production several times. Still, many thought the production was cursed. Even the director, an avowed skeptic, thought there might be supernatural influences affecting the set at Georgetown.

Georgetown is no stranger to supernatural incidents. It has ghost stories connected to it in many places on campus. In fact, many believe a student in Healy Hall accidentally opened a portal which caused the 5th floor to be sealed off. The elevator will not go to that floor any more, it always stops at the 4th floor. The school refuses to admit anything is amiss in this building or that there is a 5th floor though clearly visible from the building's exterior. Haley Hall is a 6-7 minute walk from the Exorcist Steps.

Closer to the steps, there have been reports of apparitions of Civil War soldiers from both sides. Just down the street, the ghost of noted spiritualist Mary Steele Morris has been encountered in her former home on Prospect Street. There are even accounts of paranormal activity connected to the famous steps themselves.

Activity at the Steps

Tourists, visitors, and students have claimed to see strange things at times on the steps. Shadow figures have been frequently encountered. There have also been reports of disembodied voices coming from the steps. More shocking are the claims that several people who visited the steps have died shortly after.

Stepping Up and Sharing My Final Thoughts

Report of paranormal incidents at the steps may be anecdotal or imagined. Like many of my readers, I haven't had the chance to investigate for myself. What I can say for sure is that the entire Georgetown area is a beautiful historic and haunted hot spot to visit while in the Washington DC area. There are so many ghost stories in Georgetown, they merit their own books (and there are quite a few). I need to take steps to go see these stairs for myself one day and experience the other Historic Haunts of Georgetown as well.

WASHINGTON D.C.
Historic Haunts of the North II

THE HAUNTS OF THE UNUSUAL OCTAGON HOUSE
The Octagon House, Washington DC

On an acute-angled intersection of New York Avenue, in the Foggy Bottom neighborhood of Washington D.C., sits one of the city's more unique, but lesser known historical landmarks. The Colonel John Tayloe III House, or as it is more commonly known, The Octagon House. It is one of the five houses in the country to ever serve as the Presidential Residence, The building played a key part in the War of 1812. Many in the D.C. area know it for its rich history, unusual name, and fascinating design. To others it is more readily recognized as a building with a long history of being haunted.

*Octagon House postcard
Author's Collection*

The Creation of The Octagon House

John Tayloe III was born into a wealthy family in the late 1700s on the colonial estate of Mount Airy in Richmond County, Virginia. He was educated at Eton College and Cambridge. He inherited the estate (becoming the richest Virginia planter of his time). and married Ann Ogle in 1792. The newlyweds were considering building a home in Philadelphia, but were convinced by a well-known relation, George Washington, to build in D.C. instead. At his behest the architect William Thornton (who also designed the U.S. Capitol) was secured to design them a house. It was originally meant to be a winter residence. Thus the Colonel John Tayloe II House was built between 1799 in 1801.

The brick house was built from the finest materials of the time with doors made from mahogany. It featured closets on every floor (an innovation at the time). The property also had outbuildings including a smokehouse, laundry, carriage house, slave quarters, and an ice house (the only surviving outbuilding). However, it became more well known for its fascinating floorplan, including a circular main room, six sides, and eight unusual angles. These eight angles, earned it the name it's more commonly known as, The Octagon House.

The Octagon House and the War of 1812

British forces were on the march towards Washington in 1814, and burning or destroying many buildings in their wake. Ann Ogle Tayloe, hoping to avoid the same fate for her house, offered it to the French Consulate. She hoped the fact that it would be flying a French flag outside, and the embassy's status as a "diplomatic residence" might save it. Her ploy was suc-

WASHINGTON D.C.
The Haunts of the Octagon House

cessful. As the English marched, and First Lady Dolly Madison fled the city, she too recognized the consulate's semi-protected status and had her pet parrot sent their for safe keeping.

Unfortunately, British forces burned the White House and other parts of Washington in early 1814. The only thing that stopped the British from burning and taking the city, was the sudden and eerie development of a freak weather phenomenon. From a reportedly beautiful day with blue skies and puffy clouds, a sudden and powerful tornado sprung up that struck Washington D.C. This occurred as the British were marching in to sack and burn the capitol city. This forced their retreat and marked a turning point in the war. The extreme weather event was considered by some as an act of "divine intervention" and the storm was referred to as "the tornado that saved Washington".

With the British burning raids and the passing of the tornado, the returning President and First Lady were left with an uninhabitable White House. Tayloe offered his home to Pres. James Madison and his wife Dolly for temporary use as their "Executive Mansion".The President and his wife moved in on September 8, 1814. For six months the building would serve as the Presidential Residence, during which time Dolly Madison hosted large parties on Wednesdays, called "squeezes". On February 17,1815, in the building's upstairs study, President Madison would ratify the Treaty of Ghent, thereby ending The War of 1812. After repairs were completed on the White House, President Madison and his wife left the Octagon House.

The Tayloe family moved in and lived in their supposed summer home year round from 1818 to 1855. They had 15 children. John Tayloe III died in the Octagon House in 1828. His wife Ann would remain there with the extended family until her death in the house in 1855.

The Octagon House After the Tayloes

After their parent's deaths, the Tayloe children began renting the building out. It was reportedly a hospital briefly during the Civil War, and later in the 1860s, a girl's school. The Federal government used the building in the 1870s. In the 1880s it was converted into apartments to house 10 families or individuals.

In 1898, the American Institute of Architects selected it to be their new national headquarters. They rented it for 4 years, before buying it in 1902. It would serve as the headquarters until they built a new building in 1960. It was converted and opened by the group as a museum in 1970. In the 1990s it was restored to its 1817 era appearance. Today it holds public programs, educational tours, exhibits, special events, and reportedly, ghosts!

Haunted Activity at the Octagon House

Reports of paranormal activity inside the Octagon House have been well known since the early 1800s. Apparitions and otherworldly energies have apparently been experienced in many places throughout the building (including on several different floors, the third floor bedrooms, the stairs and the

WASHINGTON D.C.
Historic Haunts of the North II

garden area in the rear). These reports have been made by the public, museum curators, and other museum employees. A museum superintendent in the 1960s claimed the active spirits in the house would often turn on the lights and open the Octagon House doors late at night.

In addition to manifesting as apparitions, the unidentified household ghosts apparently engage in other haunted activity. Curators of the museum have found traces of tiptoeing human feet in the otherwise undisturbed dust of the top floor landing. The main hallway's hanging lamp allegedly swings by itself. There is also a spot at the foot of the main staircase that people feel strangely and eerily "compelled" to avoid. Some of those who have chosen to take the stairs in the house claim to feel cold spots and weird feelings in certain areas as they ascend or descend the steps. Deathly screams have even been heard coming from inside the house as early as 1908. While no longer encountered in the house years after their removal, there have also been tales told for decades of the ghostly bells of the building.

The Ghostly Bells of the Octagon House

Some of the most enduring ghostly tales connected to the house involved the mysterious ringing of the servant's call bells. These bells were supposedly connected in some paranormal fashion to the souls of the African American slaves who used to live and work in the house. It was said the spirits of the dead slaves would make their presence known by ringing the bells loudly. This ethereal bell ringing was reportedly first encountered in the house in the early 1800s while John Tayloe was still alive. Mary Clemmer Ames wrote about it in her book;

"It is an authenticated fact, that every night at the same hour, all the bells would ring at once. One gentleman, dining with Colonel Tayloe, when this mysterious ringing began, being an unbeliever in mysteries, and a very powerful man, jumped up and caught the bell wires in his hand, but only to be lifted bodily from the floor, while he was unsuccessful in stopping the ringing. Some declare that it was discovered, after a time, that rats were the ghosts who rung the bells; others, that the cause was never discovered, and that finally the family, to secure peace, were compelled to take the bells down and hang them in different fashion. Among other remedies, had been previously tried that of exorcism, but the prayers of the priest who had been summoned availed nought."

—Mary Clemmer Ames (1874), **Ten Years in Washington: Life and Scenes in the National Capital as a Woman Sees Them.** Queen City Publishing Company

General George Ramsey was present on one particular night when the bells rang violently.

"I have been told by the daughters of General George D. Ramsay that upon one occasion their father was requested by Colonel John Tayloe...to remain at

WASHINGTON D.C.
The Haunts of the Octagon House

the Octagon overnight, when we was obliged to be absent, as a protection to his daughters... While the members of the family were at the evening meal, the bells in the house began to ring violently. General Ramsay immediately arose from the table to investigate, but failed to unravel the mystery. The butler, in a state of great alarm, rushed into the dining-room and declared that it was the work of an unseen hand. As they continued to ring, General Ramsay held the rope which controlled the bells, but, it is said, they were not silenced."
—From Marian Gouverneur (1911), *As I Remember: Recollections of American Society During the Nineteenth Century*. Appleton and Company,

The family lived with these ghost bells for several generations even after John Tayloe's death. His granddaughter was quoted discussing the bells. Virginia Tayloe Lewis' quote was featured in a book written by George McCue;

"The bells rang for a long time after my Grandfather Tayloe's death, and every one said that the house was haunted; the wires were cut and still they rang... Our dining room servant would come upstairs to ask if anyone rang the bell, and no one had."
— George McCue (1976). *The Octagon: Being an Account of a Famous Washington Residence, Its Great Years, Decline & Restoration*. Washington, D.C.: American Institute of Architects Foundation.

Eventually the spirited activity of the bells was so frequent and disturbing, that it caused them to be removed altogether from the house. For a while after, their disembodied sounds were still heard. Today the ghostly bell ringing is no longer heard, but there are other places in the house where certain restless spirits announce their presence.

The Gambler's Ghost
A gambler was reportedly shot to death in a third-floor bedroom, killed over a card game reportedly going on in the room. His ghost has often been encountered in the room. In 1912, a newspaper reported the scary and unlucky story of a man who occupied the room for a month. He was visited by the gambler's ghost nightly. While ghostly gambler's identity is unknown, other spirits in the house have seemingly been identified.

Well Hello Dolly
Dolly Madison is also said to haunt the Octagon House. She is often seen near the fireplace in the main ballroom in the garden. Many people report the smell of lilacs when she is near (it was her favorite flower). Her ghost has also been seen hosting a reception in the front hall and dining room. Perhaps she's hosting the Tayloes, the spirits most commonly reported in the Octagon House.

WASHINGTON D.C.
Historic Haunts of the North II

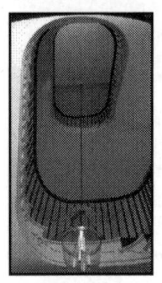

The Tayloe Family Phantoms

The ghost of John Tayloe III, the apparent paranormal patriarch of the family has been spotted throughout the house. So too has his wife Ann. However, the most commonly encountered members of the Tayloe family are two of his daughters. Legends have sprung up about the origins of their ghostly conditions and persisted for years (legends I have been unable to historically substantiate). These spectral sisters are found frequently, each in certain areas of the house.

Octagon Steps courtesy Payton Chung Creative Commons

According to these legends the first ghostly daughter had an argument with her dad over the girl's relationship with a British officer. They were standing on the second floor landing when the girl went to walk away from her father and mysteriously fell over the railing to her death. Her spirit is often seen at the bottom of the stairs and on the second floor landing. Her presence is also marked at times by the light and appearance of a ghostly candle that moves up the staircase as if being carried by someone or something unseen.

The other spectral sister's story also involves another doomed and forbidden romantic relationship. She had eloped with a man and her father was enraged when he found out. They got into an argument while on the third floor landing, she attempted to walk away from her father when she also fell over the railing just as her sister did. Her phantom form often manifests between the second and third floors. She is also sometimes encountered as a shadow figure seen on the stairs between the second and third floor or on the third floor landing.

Final Thoughts on the Spirits of The Octagon House

Whether you believe in ghosts or not, The Octagon House is a fabulous piece of Washington D.C. history. Architecture fans might be drawn to the Octagon House by the building's unique design. Six sided buildings were thought to relate to connection and communion or magical healing, six was thought by some to be the number of creation. In architecture, connection with the number eight (as in the angles of this unusual building) represented regeneration, rebirth, or renewal.

Fans of historic locations may be drawn here by the fact that it is one of only three former or current main Presidential Residences still in existence (the former presidents of course each had their own homes they left while they served, but Presidential Residences are the ones they mainly lived in while in office). Fans of Historic Haunts may be drawn here by the reports of paranormal activity or its status as one of the most haunted buildings in Washington D.C. Whatever draws you to visit this amazing building, it's sure to have an effect on you.

WASHINGTON D.C.

GHOSTS IN THE WHITE HOUSE
The White House, Washington DC

1600 Pennsylvania Avenue is quite possibly the most famous address in the world. It is the residence and workplace of the President of the United States of America. According to many Presidents, First Ladies, staffers and guests, it also claims a long history full of paranormal activity.

*The White House (North view)
Courtesy Cezary p
Wikimedia Creative Commons*

The White House Origins

Our first President George Washington selected the site where the White House stands today in 1791. The cornerstone was laid in 1792. It took eight years of construction before President John Adams and his wife Abigail moved into the unfinished president's house in 1800.

In 1801 Thomas Jefferson moved into the White House, Jefferson was prone to make architectural improvements to the buildings he lived in, The White House was no exception. Working with an architect named Latrobe, Jefferson added colonnades that concealed storage and stables in each wing.

During the War of 1812, the British set fire to the building in 1814. The fire destroyed the interior and charred much of the exterior. The damaged areas were rebuilt and President James Monroe moved in, in 1817. There were many additions made over the next several years.

*George Washington
public domain*

The South and North porticoes were added in 1824 and 1826 respectively. Teddy Roosevelt oversaw the newly made West Wing and had offices moved there in 1906. In 1908, President Taft expanded the West Wing and had the Oval Office added. The White House saw further expansion in the 1920s.

By the 1940s, it became apparent the White House needed more thorough repairs. The load-bearing walls inside were close to failing. In the late 1940s, Harry Truman had a new steel frame, constructed inside the walls and the interior rooms rebuilt

In the early 1960s. Under First Lady Jacqueline Kennedy, the interiors were extensively restored. She managed to reacquire grand art, artworks, paintings and other pieces that once resided in the White House. In her efforts, she also tried to match some of the room renovations to historical record

*White House expanded construction
public domain*

149

WASHINGTON D.C.
Historic Haunts of the North II

and modified others to match the French tastes of earlier presidents Madison and Monroe.

Each president since Kennedy has made changes or alterations to the White House interior. None of these revisions have occurred without supervisions. The Committee for the Renovation of the White House oversees all changes, well aware of the stature of this iconic building and its place in history.

So many important people have come and gone through this building and so many decisions important to our country have been made here. It is no wonder then that there might be a few spirits still haunting these historic halls. If these walls could talk, can you imagine the stories they would tell?

Stories from the Haunted White House

"I sit in this old house, all the while listening to the ghosts walk up and down the hallway. At four o'clock I was awakened by three distinct knocks on my bedroom door. No one was there. Damn place is haunted, sure as shootin'!".
—President Harry Truman (in a letter to his wife, Bess)

This wasn't Truman's only encounter. He often wrote to his wife of ghosts and ghostly encounters he experienced. In fact, he detailed one encounter at 9 p.m. on a night in 1946, where he claimed to have heard knocks and disembodied footsteps. That letter has been preserved and archived in the Presidential Library and Museum.

Harry Truman public domain

Truman wasn't alone, some eight presidents, several first-ladies, and numerous staff and guests have reported that the White House is haunted. It is considered by some to be the nation's most famous haunted house. The Washington Post even published a piece in August of 1907, detailing the extreme paranormal activity there and the prolonged effort to deal with it.

The Rose Bedroom is said to be the most haunted in the White House. The main entity believed to be haunting the area is Andrew Jackson. People have physically seen him in this room and have also heard conversations taking place when the door is closed. If you knock or open the door to see where the voices are originating from the conversation stops and the door opens to an empty room.

Jackson's ghost is often encountered cursing and swearing. First Lady Mary Todd Lincoln was a believer in spirits and held seances where she was said to have encountered Jackson's ghost. Ironic, since her husband's ghost is by far the most famous paranormal resident of the White House.

President Lincoln lost his son "Willie" at age 11 in 1862, while in the White House, (most likely of typhoid fever). Lincoln claimed to have had regular visits from the ghost of his son, as did his wife. Many people have

"Willie" Lincoln public domain

WASHINGTON D.C.
Ghosts in the White House

claimed to see the apparition of a small boy playing and giggling in the Lincoln Bedroom. Perhaps Willie was coming to warn his father.

Lincoln foresaw his own death more than once. This included a dream he had shortly before he was killed. It was was not long after his assassination that Mary Todd Lincoln reported being haunted by his ghost and reports of spiritual encounters with Lincoln began.

Lincoln's ghost has been seen traveling up and down second floor hallways. His spirit has been seen rapping on, and standing by windows. Teddy. Roosevelt frequently reported spotting Lincoln's ghost in different rooms, and in the halls. There seems to be some correlation to the frequency of his visits and times of great need or peril to our country. Further proof of this theory came during Franklin D. Roosevelt's presidency (1933-1945), when paranormal reports of Lincoln's ghost were plentiful.

Abraham Lincoln public domain

Queen Wilhelmina of the Netherlands encountered Lincoln's ghost while staying at the White House. She opened her door after hearing knocking only to come face to face with Lincoln's ghost. The Queen fainted.

Like Wilhelmina, Winston Churchill also encountered Lincoln's ghost while staying at the White House. Churchill encountered Lincoln's ghost by a fireplace after the English statesman had just stepped out of a bath wearing nothing but a cigar.

"Good evening, Mr. President", Churchill reportedly said. "You seem to have me at something of a disadvantage," Churchill continued. Lincoln's ghost reportedly smiled and vanished.

Grace Coolidge (Calvin's wife and First Lady) witnessed Lincoln's ghost looking out his old office window. President Lincoln is also often seen looking out the window of his old bedroom. He seems to be staring off, possibly still trying to make the right decisions for his country. Many think he returned after his death because he still feels there's work to do.

Winston Churchill public domain

In addition to Lincoln's ghost, the apparition of iconic American female and First Lady Dolly Madison has also been seen. Her spirit is most often encountered in the gardens. She loved the gardens, maybe a little too much. Dolly seems to get very upset when someone tries to make changes to the gardens and she lets the gardeners known about it. There is a photo inside the White House of Dolly, and people who have encountered her spirit say she looks just like the picture. The vast majority of paranormal reports involving Dolly Madison's ghost have been made by the White House gardening staff.

One of my favorite ghosts at the White House is Mrs. Abigail Adams. She is often seen walking through the hallway carrying something. Some who have seen her say it looks like a basket full of laundry. It wouldn't surprise me if the ghost of this strong woman with an opinion on everything was still

151

WASHINGTON D.C.
Historic Haunts of the North II

here. Possibly overseeing things, or maybe even sharing her opinions with the more recent presidents, as she did with John. John Adams would often discuss important matters with Abigail because he felt she always had good ideas and could see things outside of the box.

Outside the box is an apt description for where the last few human spirits of the White House are encountered. The ghost of David Burns (who sold the land White House now sits on) has been heard in the Oval Office. Thomas Jefferson's ghost has reportedly been heard playing violin. The ghost of Anne Surratt has been encountered supposedly frantically knocking on the White House front door begging for her mother Mary's life (an accused accomplice in Lincoln's assassination). The spirit of an unknown 14-15 year old boy has been known to scare housekeepers, (especially during Taft's presidency). The staff referred to him as "the Thing". He's not the only "thing" to have haunted these venerable walls.

Clinton Eastroom where Abigail Adams' ghost has been seen with Laundry public domain

DC, the "Demon Cat"

The last spirit I want to tell you about is known as "DC". Some say DC stands for Demon Cat and others say it's for the District of Columbia. DC is a phantom black cat who has predicted some of the nation's worst events. He is said to appear just before presidential elections and tragic events take place. Paranormal reports claim DC appeared before the 1920's stock market crash, before John F. Kennedy's assassination, and even before September 11th. There are even some reports that claim he appeared in 1865, the morning Lincoln was killed. Witnesses claim "DC" appears as a normal cat, but swells to the size of a giant tiger or elephant when it has discovered that it's spotted or being watched. It usually then reacts in one of two ways. It moves to "pounce" on the witnesses vanishing into thin air just before making contact. In other stories, "DC" explodes and disappears. This is not a spirit you want to come in contact with or even see, a black cat who's path you definitely don't want to cross.

Parting Thoughts

Someone asked me a few years ago if I could ask the previous presidents a question, what would I ask them? Silly question perhaps, I would ask, "So, what ghosts did you come in contact with at the White House?" I encourage everyone to visit this historic site. Whether you experience anything at the White House or not, stories of paranormal activity have been going on for well over 200 years! America's Executive Mansion is a must for any true fan of Historic Haunts.

WASHINGTON D.C.
Ghosts in the White House

The Resolute Desk

Resolute Desk recreation public domain

While not typically the subject of intense ghost stories, a variety of legends have arisen about the President's desk (for example in the *National Treasure* movies). Over the years it has taken on an iconic status of it's own. No mention of the White House would be complete without mentioning this ornate piece of American history.

The resolute desk is a 19th century Planter's Desk used by several presidents in the Oval Office. The desk was a gift from Queen Victoria to President Hayes in 1880. The desk was built from English oak timbers found on the British Arctic explorer ship HMS Resolute. Resolute was part of an expedition, sent in search of Sir John Franklin in 1852. It was abandoned in May of 1854. In September of 1855, the ship was discovered and freed from the ice by Captain Boddington of the United States whaler "George Henry". The ship was purchased, fitted, and returned to England as a gift to Queen Victoria, by the President and people of the United States.

This was done to ease escalating tensions and as a gesture of friendship and goodwill. When the ship was broken up, after being decommissioned in 1879, the table was made from her timbers along with two matching writing tables. One for Queen Victoria and the "Connell" Desk (named for and given to the man who helped recover and outfit the Resolute). It has proudly been used by most heads of state since Hayes' time.

There are some stories connected to the desk and the possibility of secret compartments or paranormal activity (no surprise perhaps with the Resolute having experienced some chilling circumstances). However, most people associate the desk with the pictures of the presidents and the documents signed upon it. Despite the often serious nature of the oval office around this desk, Kennedy allowed his children to play in and around it creating yet another batch of iconic stories involving this historic desk.

President Barack Obama and then–Vice President (later President) Joe Biden discuss the desk with Charles III, then Prince of Wales, and Camilla, then Duchess of Cornwall, in 2015. Public Domain image

153

WEST VIRGINIA

A PARANORMAL WITNESS FOR THE PROSECUTION, THE GREENBRIER GHOST

Greenbrier Ghost, Sam Black Church, West Virginia

A few miles west of Lewisburg, West Virginia stands a noteworthy state highway mile marker. It details not only a part of Appalachian history, but a unique case in the American judicial system. The marker near Sam Black Church tells readers of the Greenbrier Ghost case. The "Only known case in which testimony from a ghost helped convict a murderer". So claims the Greenbrier Ghost Trail Marker. The ghost in question is that of Mrs. Elva Zona Heaster Shue.

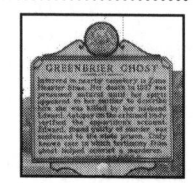

Green Brier Ghost Marker

The History and the Murder

Elva or "Zona" as most called her was a popular member of the local community despite having a child out of wedlock in 1895. So it was a surprise to some when she met a stranger, a drifter named Edward Shue and got swept up in a whirlwind romance late in 1896. Edward drew attention by being new to the region, but certainly was also a stand out due to his charm, charisma, good looks, and boastful nature. Zona was swept off her feet and the two were married. Zona's mother, Mary Jane Heaster, objected to the marriage and didn't trust Edward.

Zona Heaster public domain

It wasn't long before Zona was expecting a child. Unfortunately, just as their courtship and marriage was unusual, this too would not be a normal pregnancy. Zona was seen several times by Dr. George Knapp for numerous health issues. Knapp would record these incidents and mysterious ailments with euphemisms like "female complaint".

On the morning of January 23, 1897, Edward who was working as a blacksmith, sent Andy Jones an 11 year old neighbor who did chores and odd jobs to his house on an errand. He discovered Zona's body at the bottom of the staircase leading to the second floor where she lived with her husband of three months. She was found with her feet together and one hand on her stomach. Andy ran and told his mother, then ran to the blacksmith's shop where Edward worked.

Edward was described as being in great anguish when he heard the news. He ran to his home and reportedly swept his dead wife into his arms. He asked for someone to send word to Zona's doctor and the local coroner, Dr.

154

WEST VIRGINIA
The Greenbrier Ghost

George Knapp. It took Knapp an hour and a half to arrive. By the time Knapp arrived, Edward had dressed his dead wife's body in a high-necked gown with a scarf around her neck and a veil over her face. Edward would let no one handle the body. In fact, he acted violently when Knapp wished to more clearly examine the body. As a result, Knapp gave the body only a cursory look due to Edward's grief and anguish.

Zona's body was brought to her mother's house to prepare for burial. Edward always remained at the corner of the casket and prepared the body. He once again dressed her in high-necked outfit with a scarf he said was her favorite. Some spectators claimed Zona's head seemed oddly loose. Perhaps in response, Edward put sheets on either side of her head and would let no one else touch the body. During the wake, it was reported that Edward's demeanor ranged from overwhelming sadness to incredible energy. Zona's body was laid to rest at Soule Chapel Methodist Cemetery. Dr. Knapp would record her cause of death at first as "everlasting faint" (a heart attack), but would later record it officially as a death from childbirth.

The Unusual Activity Begins

Many in the community were saddened by Zona's death, but knowing the doctor had seen her many times before, thought nothing was amiss. Others in the community thought things seemed a little odd or didn't add up, Zona's mother was among them. At the funeral and before the burial, Mary removed the sheets that were beside her daughter's head and tried to return them to Edward. He repeatedly refused. Mary noticed an odd odor coming from the sheets. She tried to wash them and the basin turned red when she put the sheets in, the sheet itself turned pink and the water cleared. Mary discovered to her dismay that the stains in the sheet could not be removed.

It was known that Mary did not believe in ghosts, yet she prayed every night fervently for weeks after the burial asking her daughter's spirit to return and tell her what happened. About a month after the burial and over the course of four consecutive nights, Mary apparently got her wish. Zona's spirit reportedly returned appearing at Mary's bedside. The apparition at first appeared as a bright light which gradually took shape and changed form to that of her daughter.

All four times Mary saw her daughter she was wearing the same dress she died in and told her mother that Edward had come home from work and in anger (supposedly over the lack of meat in his dinner) broke her neck in a fit of rage. Edward was a blacksmith and there is no doubt he was strong enough to have done it. Zona's spirit emphasized that point to her mother by reportedly turning her head around until it faced backwards!

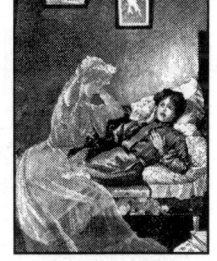

Zona's ghost appears illustration public domain

The Aftermath of the Ghostly Visits

Mary Heaster and her brother went to John Preston, a prosecuting attorney

155

WEST VIRGINIA
Historic Haunts of the North II

for Greenbrier County. Preston was skeptical at first, but could not help being swayed by her story and her conviction in the telling of it. Preston contacted the coroner Dr. Knapp. Knapp agreed he could have been mistaken with his diagnosis especially given the intense events of that day, and his lack of intense scrutiny of the body. This was enough for Preston.

The court ordered the body to be exhumed, an autopsy performed and a formal inquest to begin. Edward Shue vigorously protested this course of action. He was told he would be forced to attend the inquest. He reportedly replied that he knew he would be arrested, but they would be unable to prove he did it. Three doctors performed the autopsy. Upon examining poor Zona's body more closely, they discovered her neck had, in fact, been broken and she had suffered a smashed windpipe. Further, they discovered the marks of fingers where she had been choked. Shue was arrested and charged with murder.

During the trial other details emerged about Edward's questionable past. He had been married twice before and at least one of them had died of unusual circumstances from a broken neck. Edward had also been a criminal having served in a penitentiary before. The prosecution of course brought these details to the forefront while hoping to downplay the details of Zona's ghostly visits. In fact, they didn't even call Mary to testify, it was the defense that brought her to the stand to tell her tale. Mary Jane Heaster, to her credit, never waiverd or varied her accounts of the four nights despite intense badgering by Edward's lawyer under cross-examination. On June 22nd, 1897 a jury found Shue guilty. Newspapers and court officials claimed he was found guilty largely because of circumstantial evidence and not the details from Zona's ghostly testimony. Edward was sent to prison and moved ultimately to the West Virginia Penitentiary in Moundsville (after a failed attempt to Lynch him).

Edward only served eight years at the state prison when he was found dead under mysterious circumstances. Men who murder women aren't looked upon too well by other prisoners. Maybe the prisoners took care of his sentence in Zona's honor?

The Greenbrier County Courthouse, where Edward was on trial can still be seen today. The court records are still on file with Zona's "ghostly testimony" relayed through her mother. Mary Jane Heaster never recanted her story even unto her death in 1916. Zona's ghost was never seen again by her mother or anyone else after the guilty verdict. Although the area is not known to be haunted today, it is still a great piece of paranormal history where a ghost may have been the reason a murderer was brought to justice in a court of law. To this day this remains one of the most popular ghostly tales of the area, and the marker is a testament to one heck of a Historic Haunt!

WEST VIRGINIA

FRIGHTENING ENCOUNTERS AT THE ABANDONED AMUSEMENT PARK

Lake Shawnee Amusement Park, Princeton, WV

When you hear the phrase "Amusement Park" you think, fun, laughter, rides, popcorn, and great memories. Unfortunately, at one particular former amusement park in Mercer County, near Princeton, West Virginia, it's hard to separate the amusing from the alarming, and the spooky from the supernatural. The former Lake Shawnee Amusement Park is unique among the multitude of abandoned amusement parks in the United States. Let's take a closer look at the shocking history of misfortune that has indelibly marked this location as one of the "scariest places in America".

Entrance to property
Forsaken Fotos
Creative Commons

The History of the Lake Shawnee Area

Long before the coming of European Settlers and their descendants, this area was sacred land to the Native Americans. The Shawnee had inhabited the region for centuries. They were still under the impression that this was their land when the Clay family came to live here.

Mitchell Clay, a veteran of The Battle of Point Pleasant (see Cornstalk's Curse in **Historic Haunts of the North**), came here with his wife Phoebe in 1775. They had acquired a large segment of this land which at the time was called Cloverbottom. They were reportedly, the first settlers of Mercer County. Here they built a homestead intending to raise their children (they would have 14). In 1783, Clay was out hunting with one of his older sons. A Native American raiding party approached his property. Two of the Clay children were killed and scalped. A third Clay child was kidnapped and taken to nearby Chillicothe where he was later burned at the stake. Clay, wanting revenge, gathered a posse of the nearby landowners to track down the Native Americans. They traveled a distance before catching up to them. Clay and his group massacred the bulk of the Native American raiding party. The traumatized Clay Family would sell their land and return to Pearisburg to live out their lives with their remaining children. After the incident the land was considered by many to be "cursed". The incident affected the community so much that they erected a monument commemorating the family's misfortune at the Mercer County Courthouse. The statue is called "Agony in Stone". Over a century would pass, the story would become part of local legend, and

157

WEST VIRGINIA
Historic Haunts of the North II

the property would change hands several times.

In 1926, the property was purchased by Conley Trigg Snidow, Sr., an entrepreneur. Snidow was familiar with the property's tragic history, but with its position at the intersection of two main roads, he saw possibility in this location. He began the process of developing the land to create an amusement park for the people of Mercer County.

Lake Shawnee Amusement Park opened in 1926, on land that once witnessed part of the Clay family being killed by local Native Americans. The amusement park featured a ferris wheel, swing ride, racetrack, dance hall, speakeasy, concession stand, and cabins for guests that wanted to stay overnight. It also featured a large pond which was divided to include a concrete built pool with a slide. The park became very popular among the local residents, especially the families of coal miners in the area. By the 1950s, Lake Shawnee Amusement Park had added hiking trails, a golf driving range, shooting range, and additional cottages and cabins (taking the total to 16). It continued to be popular with patrons, but reported incidents of life-threatening misfortune began to circulate. These "accidents" would ultimately prove deadly for some and stir up controversy again about the "cursed" status of the land.

Ferris Wheel
Forsaken Fotos
Creative Commons

The Accidents Take Lives

Several visitors to Lake Shawnee reported unusual episodes in the park. Some guests described feeling as if something was tugging at them from below in the concrete swimming pool. Many people believed that there was "something" or some force in the pool and pond that could pull people down to their death. Despite this, the pool and pond were open for swimming and a little boy mysteriously drowned. Later, a second, slightly older boy, drown in the pool, apparently after being sucked into the powerful drain. Unfortunately, these two deaths would draw even more attention to the swimming areas. The pool was closed and closed in. However, the accidents wouldn't stop there.

The Pond
Forsaken Fotos
Creative Commons

The Girl on the Swing and Others

While the park was operating one day, a young girl in pink was happily swaying on the giant swing. A local delivery vehicle sent to drop off Soda Pop slid nearby in the mud. The little girl in her pink dress was struck and killed by the delivery truck. The bloodied body of the little girl was a disturbing reminder of the accidents the park kept having.

Swings
Forsaken Fotos
Creative Commons

WEST VIRGINIA
Lake Shawnee Amusement Park

Another fatal accident supposedly occurred involving a car and a person on the road just outside the property (on Route 19 which runs adjacent to the park). The situation seems to have been described as a hit and run by some, a murder by others. In total, at least six strange deaths were tied to this area. Multiple other non-fatal incidents also happened at the park, but were handled and dealt with (as most amusement parks do).

The End of Lake Shawnee Amusement Park

By the mid 1960s, the park had started to become dilapidated and run down. The elderly owners of the park seemed to have little to no interest in continuing. After the drownings and other accidents, the heartbroken owners were even less inclined to continue operating. Alternate ideas were introduced for the property.

Wheeler College presented research suggesting its possible development as a state historic park. In 1966, another plan was proposed involving the state purchasing the property, to repurpose as a regional Boy Scout's center. Before any of these plans could be considered, however, the Mercer County Health Department closed Lake Shawnee down after violations of West Virginia's Department of Health safety codes in 1967.

After the Closure

The park sat abandoned for many years. That would change in 1985. A former park employee, Gaylord White, purchased the property. He had high hopes of restoring and renewing the park, and returning it to the community as a place of amusement. White reopened Lake Shawnee Amusement Park in the summer of 1987. Sadly, the park would once again close a few years later due to high insurance rates. White was forced to try to find other uses for the property.

In the early 1990s, White's crew was working on a part of the property when they uncovered numerous Native American artifacts on property. Archaeologists from Marshall University began working with White and his staff. Together, they uncovered artifacts for years and eventually, graves. A total of 13 Native American skeletons were uncovered, most were children. Based on what they found, there was also speculation that there may have been hundreds or thousands more on site from the days when the Shawnee claimed ownership. The land itself seems to echo the Shawnee desire to reclaim the property, as wild vegetation seems to continue to creep up and overgrow Gaylord White's old amusement park.

Gaylord passed away in 2014 of cancer. His son Chris became the caretaker of the amusement park site and the property. Besides the archeologists, in an effort to learn more about the place, Chris has hosted investigative groups, standard and paranormal. He has also invited psychics and sensitives with these groups and on their own to come. After input from some of these groups, he has taken steps intended to address the sources of possible paranormal activity there. Monuments stand at the site where the Clay children were killed. Visitors to the property are also now encouraged to leave an

WEST VIRGINIA
Historic Haunts of the North II

offering to the Shawnee.

Today the old amusement park seems to have made peace to some degree with its haunted history. Lake Shawnee Amusement Park hosts paranormal tours, overnight stays, and even a "Dark Carnival" closer to Halloween. Visitors during these outings, may discover the paranormal activity going on for themselves.

Paranormal Activity at the Old Amusement Park

We'll start with a look at the more generic and recurring incidents of activity on property. There are abundant reports of unusual sensory activity on property. Disembodied or intangible sounds like footsteps, mysterious chanting, children's voices (engaged in talking or play), and the unnerving feeling that your being followed (especially on the spooky trail leading to the Clay children's graves). Some have even reported feeling an extreme pressure on their chests, as if something were pushing on it. Others describe physically being pushed as if by some phantasmal force. While it may be easy to chalk some of this up to active imaginations (and quite a bit could be); several individuals seem to have captured some of this activity with their equipment.

Photographs taken on property often seem to develop or appear with unexplained shapes, orbs of light, and even phantom forms, that resemble faces. Some of this might be written off as "matrixing", the brain's ability to "see" a figure or face in a photograph when none may actually be present. Even acknowledging that, other images seem far more compelling and less like matrixing. Large amounts of EVPs and EMF readings have been known to register here, even in places with no electrical, natural, or man-made reasons to account for them.

Even more unsettling perhaps, are the accounts of moving shadow forms among the amusement park's old rides (especially among the ferris wheel carts). Visitors have described being "locked" in the old ticket booth and forcefully unable to open the door and get out, even though the doors don't lock! Some even claim to have been forcefully "thrown" out of certain areas on property. There have even been frequent reports of a mysteriously thick fog that seems to roll in unnaturally once night falls. The fog seem-

Ticket Booth?
Forsaken Fotos
Creative Commons

ingly provides cover for increased paranormal activity. Sounds like something straight out of a horror movie. Just like some of those horror movies, visitors camping on property have gotten so scared with this eerie weather phenomenon and what comes after, that they've left in the middle of the night, terrified.

While the reports made by witnesses of some of this unusual activity differ drastically, there are some common characteristics that seem to keep coming up. Those coming to the property without the proper and healthy respect for it, especially those coming with less than serious intentions (such as people coming to goof around, party, or litter everywhere) tend to have far more horrifying experiences on site. Even when dealing with the same suspected spirits.

In addition, people with Native American heritage or blood, generally don't seem to have as many frightening experiences (another coincidence perhaps). Certain offerings made by guests to the Shawnee (especially tobacco among others) seems to solicit strange reactions in the surrounding environment. Coyotes for example, who figure prominently in many Native American stories of religion and mythology, have been known to gather in unusually large numbers in the area after these types of offerings, and begin to engage in mad howling as a group.

There have even been multiple encounters with Native American apparitions on site. This includes Native American spirits, some seven feet tall, that are spotted rising up from the pond. The ephemeral forms of these Tribal warriors have also been spotted on other parts of the property. They've even been spotted on property in the owner's house.

The Known "Unknown" Spirits on Site

The first "known" spirit is experienced at the outskirts of the property, A lingering presence, connected somehow to the fatal incident on the road that runs adjacent to the park, has been encountered. This spirit seems more residual than interactive.

The spirits of the two poor young souls who drown in the pool are also encountered there. Witnesses describe a young boy's ghost that has repeatedly manifested, appearing soaking wet, near the pool/pond area. These "ghost boys" have been seen elsewhere on site as well.

The spectral spirit of another boy has been seen on site (one of the Clay boys perhaps). This one seems to have decided to protect the innocent guests who visit the old amusement park. He's been known to hold or gently push these visitors away from the more eerily active hotspots on sight. Places like the ferris wheel where the menacing shadow forms are encountered, and even the swings. Still, the swings are believed to be the origin of the most common and interactive spirit on site, the little girl in pink who died on them.

Ferris Wheel closeup
Forsaken Fotos
Creative Commons

The Unfortunate Little Girl on the Swings

The apparition of the little girl in pink is encountered at times randomly throughout the park. Her phantom has been seen on a tractor in the park (which was left purposely in place after her first appearance for years). She has also reportedly been seen near the road. Her materialization is typically marked by playful interactions with the living. Those subjected to her visits, all but a select few, describe her as a pretty little girl dressed in pink. However, some have supposedly encountered her spirit matted in blood, as she was on the day of the accident that killed her (perhaps these few did not

161

WEST VIRGINIA
Historic Haunts of the North II

have the purest of motivations for seeking her out). For these unfortunate eyewitnesses, the appearance of her bloodied corpse seems to leave them transfixed and unable to move, until she leaves or dissipates.

Of course the girl in pink's insubstantial spirit is most often seen near the swings that marked her final moments. Besides the little girl, the swings themselves seem to exhibit some suggestive paranormal activity. The swing the little girl died in has a propensity for unusual cold spots (even on the hottest days) and seems to move on its own. The former owner of the place, Gaylord White, frequently heard the swings creaking as they were unnaturally in motion, and saw them moving when there was no one there to push them and no wind sufficient enough to cause them to move. Not surprising, ghost hunting equipment often seems to go wild with activity near the swing.

So What Do the "Sensitives" Say

Many psychics or those calling themselves "sensitives" have visited Lake Shawnee. Their statements seem to suggest they're receiving the same messages from "beyond the veil". They describe a "bad vibe" that the property has. The Native American spirits seem to let them know in various ways that the land is sacred and they generally don't want people there.

The sensitives also claim that the Native American spirits have the ability to project problems onto the living to get them to leave. The brother of the current caretaker, Chris White, who frequently worked on property and gave tours, had heart attacks in the double digits before he passed. Coincidence perhaps.

The sensitives have also divulged their beliefs that the Native American spirits can project bad emotions into others to encourage them to leave invoking anger, sowing discourse. These clairvoyants claim the tribal spirits have even learned to more physically interact with the surrounding area at times, and have. This is a disturbing thought.

My Final Thoughts

It's hard not to think something supernatural might be going on at the park. Several paranormal television shows have filmed here and many of them have had personal paranormal experiences. While the restless spirits at the park may wish these investigators (and people in general) gone, it seems as though they may not get their wish anytime soon. The place has been extremely busy the last several years, with would-be investigators, curiosity seekers, and others coming to the former amusement park. Its popularity has only increased recently with online mentions, podcasts, and a slew of streaming content and shows (especially in the U.K. and Canada). As a descendant of these First Americans, I want to respect the place, as a paranormal investigator, I'm intrigued. This is one unique Historic Haunt. If you feel compelled to find out for yourself, contact them for a tour and you might experience something. If you go, please be respectful, and perhaps make an offering in their name.

WEST VIRGINIA

THE EERIE INMATES OF WEST VIRGINIA PENITENTIARY

West Virginia State Penitentiary, Moundsville, West Virginia

There are many paranormal cases that involve spirits who are unable to pass on, prisoners on this plane of existence. Every once in a while there is a historic site which is markedly different from most of the others. The West Virginia State Penitentiary is one of those and raises questions about what happens when the souls trapped here in life are now trapped here in death.

postcard West Virginia Penitentiary

The Penitentiary's Back Story

After an inmate escape in 1865 forced West Virginia legislators to look at constructing a state prison, acreage in Moundsville was purchased and planning began. A gothic revival style of architecture was chosen to mirror the northern Illinois Penitentiary in Joliet and to suggest to incoming prisoners - through its large looming walls and dark appearance - the misery yet to come. Construction on the main areas of West Virginia State Penitentiary started in 1867 and was completed with prison labor in 1876. Work began afterwards on the secondary facilities.

To keep the prison running and mostly self-sufficient, there were a few industries established within the prison walls using inmate laborers. There was a carpentry shop, bakery, stone yard, paint shop, brickyard, blacksmith, tailor, and a hospital. The prison even had a coal mine about a mile down the street which saved them thousands of dollars every year on energy bills.

Education was even provided for the inmates in hopes of rehabilitating them. In the beginning, the prison's conditions were acceptable, it was clean, and it wasn't over populated. In addition, the food was actually decent

163

WEST VIRGINIA
Historic Haunts of the North II

(according to inmates reports). Unfortunately, by the 1920s the prison started to decline and over population began. They decided to expand the prison and attempt to stem the beginning of overpopulation before it got out of hand. That worked for a while. Eventually the situation grew worse, and new unflattering details of the jail emerged. It became evident something would need to be done about West Virginia's State Pen.

Among the stories to emerge over the years were the 36 homicides in the prison and 94 executions from 1899 till 1959, 85 of them were hangings. The last hanging turned macabre when the inmate didn't strangle to death, but was instead decapitated! Because of this the prison decided that hangings were inhumane and the electric chair should be brought in.

On October 8th, 1929, R.D. Wall was brutally murdered by three other inmates for "snitching." The culprits used dull objects as shivs and brutally beat and stabbed Wall till he finally bled to death. As time went on it became obvious too that the security of the prison wasn't what it should be. The cell doors had been picked so many times it was fairly easy to get out of the jail cells. It was becoming known as a Con's Prison. It was even listed on the U.S. Department of Justice's Top Ten Most Violent Correctional Facilities list.

In November 1979, 15 inmates escaped, and then on January 1st, 1986 a riot broke out. With serious overcrowding issues and lack of efficient guards, it was extremely easy for 20 inmates to start the riot. Unfortunately for them, the rioters didn't really have a plan, just a list of demands about changing conditions at the penitentiary. The standoff ended up being a two day event and three inmates wound up dead. The prisoners for all their reasons really didn't accomplish anything. Within nine years of the riot, the prison closed down (1995). It just wasn't doing its job. Poor security, overcrowding, and unsanitary conditions were all reasons that disease spread throughout the prison. These were all cited as reasons for its closure.

Incidents of the Paranormal at the Pen

The cruel and unusual conditions at West Virginia State Penitentiary might explain why the prison is haunted today. Several former inmates are reportedly still haunting their cells. Numerous reports of hushed voices and the sounds of whispers are heard coming from the cell blocks, but when investigated, they stop. It's almost as if the otherworldly inmates were planning an escape. These reports are nothing new; guards at the facility were reporting unusual occurrences as early as the 1930s!

These occurrences continue to this day. Cell doors are often heard slowly creaking open or slamming shut, a phenomenon that has even been captured on video. In this case there are no air sources to explain the door's sudden movement. Further, lights go on and off of their own accord and cold spots

164

are often encountered. When people are touring the building, they also hear the sounds of heavy footsteps behind them. When they turn to see who is there they find nothing but empty space.

But perhaps the most startling and frequent paranormal experience at the prison is the shadow figures seen moving and captured in photos. People have often claimed to catch a glimpse of something out of the corner of their eye. When they turn to see what's causing it there's nothing there. Even worse, sometimes they turn to see what's there and they spy a shadow of what appears to be a large man staring at them. The prison guards referred to these shadows as "phantom inmates"! The guards also described one "shadow man" in particular that wandered the premises.

These phantoms and shadows as well as the other frequently encountered activity have earned this penitentiary a reputation as one of the most haunted prisons in the US. Indeed, several paranormal themed television shows have filmed here over the last few years. Most of these have captured startling and similar evidence of paranormal activity at the Moundsville facility, especially of the shadow figures that turns up frequently on their equipment.

For fans of the paranormal or just history, the prison is now open for historic tours by day and haunted tours by night. Many visitors have said that night fall is always the creepiest at the prison and that you never know who might be lurking around the corner watching you. Is it your shadow moving or something else?

ABOUT THE AUTHOR

Dr. Jamie Pearce

Dr. Jamie Pearce lives in the Jacksonville, Florida area with her husband Deric and their 3 cats. With over 25 years of experience in the paranormal field and six books under her belt, Jamie Pearce is obviously a fan of the paranormal.

However, she has a passion for more than history and the paranormal, she is also a scuba diver and avid runner. As a child she wanted to be a marine biologist and a fitness trainer. Even though her career path went in a different direction, she still has a passion for the ocean and being fit.

Another passion of hers is traveling and she has many new locations in mind for the future that she and her husband will hopefully be visiting. Ideally they will be featured in upcoming books. Pearce currently has four more books in the Historic Haunts series in progress (as well as others) and is always looking for new and exciting haunted locations. She continues to post the evidence of her investigations and research of the paranormal through her website **www.historic-haunts.net** and with her team **Historic Haunts Investigations. She can also be connected to on Facebook:**
www.facebook.com/HistoricHaunts
www.facebook.com/AuthorJamiePearce

Member of:
Rhine Research Center
Society for Psychical Research U.K.
Edgar Cayce A.R.E.
Ghost Club (oldest paraclub in the world)

The following pages are for your own notes on the locations listed.
We hope you will visit them and explore for yourself.

Made in the USA
Columbia, SC
06 February 2025